Math
Expressions

Volume 1

Developed by
The Children's Math Worlds Research Project

PROJECT DIRECTOR AND AUTHOR
Dr. Karen C. Fuson

This material is based upon work supported by the
National Science Foundation
under Grant Numbers
ESI-9816320, REC-9806020, and RED-935373.

Any opinions, findings, and conclusions, or recommendations expressed in this material
are those of the author and do not necessarily reflect the views of the National Science Foundation.

HOUGHTON MIFFLIN HARCOURT

Teacher Reviewers

Kindergarten
Patricia Stroh Sugiyama
Wilmette, Illinois

Barbara Wahle
Evanston, Illinois

Grade 1
Sandra Budson
Newton, Massachusetts

Janet Pecci
Chicago, Illinois

Megan Rees
Chicago, Illinois

Grade 2
Molly Dunn
Danvers, Massachusetts

Agnes Lesnick
Hillside, Illinois

Rita Soto
Chicago, Illinois

Grade 3
Jane Curran
Honesdale, Pennsylvania

Sandra Tucker
Chicago, Illinois

Grade 4
Sara Stoneberg Llibre
Chicago, Illinois

Sheri Roedel
Chicago, Illinois

Grade 5
Todd Atler
Chicago, Illinois

Leah Barry
Norfolk, Massachusetts

Special Thanks

Special thanks to the many teachers, students, parents, principals, writers, researchers, and work-study students who participated in the Children's Math Worlds Research Project over the years.

Credits

Cover art: (t) © G.K. Hart/Vikki Hart/Getty Images, (b) Photodisc/Getty Images

Illustrative art: Ginna Magee and Burgandy Beam/Wilkinson Studio; Eli Nicolosi, Geoff Smith, John Kurtz, Robin Boyer, Ron Mahoney, Tim Johnson
Technical art: Anthology, Inc.

VOLUME 1 CONTENTS

* This lesson consists only of activities from the Teacher Edition.

VOLUME 1 CONTENTS (CONTINUED)

Unit 3 Teen Numbers as Tens and Ones

* This lesson consists only of activities from the Teacher Edition.

* This lesson consists only of activities from the Teacher Edition.

Dear Family:

Your child is learning math in an innovative program that weaves abstract mathematical concepts with the everyday experiences of children. This helps children understand math better.

Your child will have homework. He or she needs a **Homework Helper.** The helper may be anyone—you, an older brother or sister (or other family member), a neighbor, or a friend. Make a specific time for homework and provide your child with a quiet place to work (for example, no TV). Encourage your child to talk about what is happening in math class. If your child is having problems with math, please talk to the teacher to see how you might help.

Thank you! You are vital to your child's learning.

Sincerely,
Your child's teacher

- -

Please fill out the following information and return this form to the teacher.

My child _____ will have _____

               (child's name)   (Homework Helper's name)

as his or her Homework Helper. This person is my child's

_____.

(relationship to child: father,
mother, sibling, friend, etc.)

Introduce Number and Counting Routines **1**

Carta a la familia

Estimada familia:

Su niño está aprendiendo matemáticas con un programa innovador que relaciona conceptos matemáticos abstractos con la experiencia diaria de los niños. Esto ayuda a los niños a entender mejor las matemáticas.

Su niño tendrá tarea y necesita a una persona que lo ayude. Esa persona puede ser usted, un hermano mayor (u otro familiar), un vecino o un amigo. Establezca una hora para la tarea y ofrezca a su niño un lugar tranquilo donde trabajar (por ejemplo un lugar sin TV). Anime a su niño a comentar lo que está aprendiendo en la clase de matemáticas. Si su niño tiene problemas con las matemáticas, por favor hable con el maestro para ver cómo usted puede ayudar.

Muchas gracias. Usted es imprescindible en el aprendizaje de su niño.

Atentamente,
El maestro de su niño

Por favor escriba la siguiente información y devuelva este formulario al maestro.

La persona que ayudará a mi niño _____ es
(nombre del niño)

_____ . Esta persona es _____
(nombre de la persona)   (relación con el niño)

de mi niño.

Introduce Number and Counting Routines

1	2	3	4	5	6
1	**2**	**3**	**4**	**5**	**6**

7	8	9	10
7	**8**	**9**	**10**

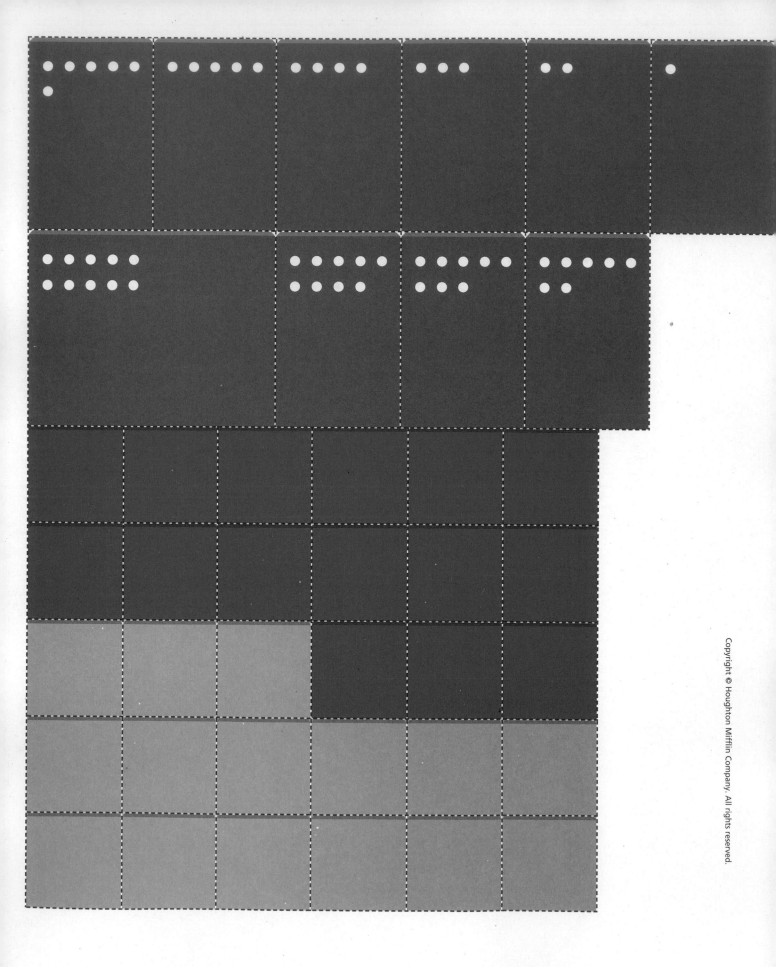

Number Tiles and Square-Inch Tiles

Dear Family:

Your child has just read and discussed *Anno's Counting Book.* This book is an introduction to beginning numbers. It is filled with charming scenes that show many things all of the same number (for example, a scene showing many different groups of 3 things). Each page shows a month of the year.

We have discussed what a scene is in class. *A scene is a place where some action or event occurs, a picture.* The children will be making their own scenes or pictures. Sometimes this will be started in class and completed for homework. You can help by talking with your child about what he or she might draw, for example, your child might draw 2 of something, such as things found in a kitchen—2 plates, 2 bowls, 2 spoons.

Help your child practice counting things in daily life. Children might count how many stairs there are in your home, how many plates you need to set the table, or how many people are in the family.

Thank you for helping your child learn more about numbers and counting!

Sincerely,
Your child's teacher

Estimada familia:

Su niño acaba de leer y comentar un libro para contar. Este libro es una introducción a los primeros números. Está lleno de escenas fascinantes que muestran muchas cosas, todas acerca de los mismos números (por ejemplo, una escena muestra varios grupos diferentes de 3 cosas). Cada página indica un mes del año.

Hemos comentado en clase lo que es una escena. *Una escena es un lugar donde ocurre una acción o un suceso, un dibujo.* Los niños van a hacer sus propias escenas o dibujos. A veces los empezarán en clase y los terminarán de tarea. Usted puede ayudar hablando con su niño sobre lo que puede dibujar. Por ejemplo: si va a dibujar 2 de algo, podría dibujar cosas que están en la cocina, 2 platos, 2 tazones, 2 cucharas.

Ayude a su niño a practicar contando cosas que usen a diario. Los niños pueden contar cuántas escaleras hay en su casa, cuántos platos se necesitan para poner la mesa o cuántas personas hay en la familia.

¡Gracias por ayudar a su niño a aprender más sobre los números y a contar!

Atentamente,
El maestro de su niño

Pattern Blocks: Hexagons and Trapezoids **7**

Pattern Blocks: Hexagons and Trapezoids

Class Activity

Name _____

Draw 5 hats.	Draw 3 cats.
Draw 4 stars.	Draw 2 cars.

➡ **On the Back** Draw 3 flowers and draw 3 trees.

Scenes of 2 and 3: Practice Visual Imagery

Name _____

Write the numbers.

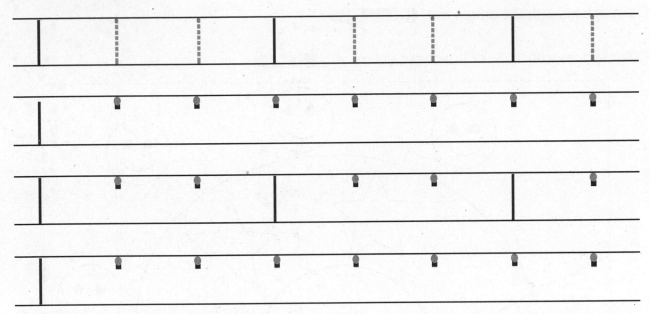

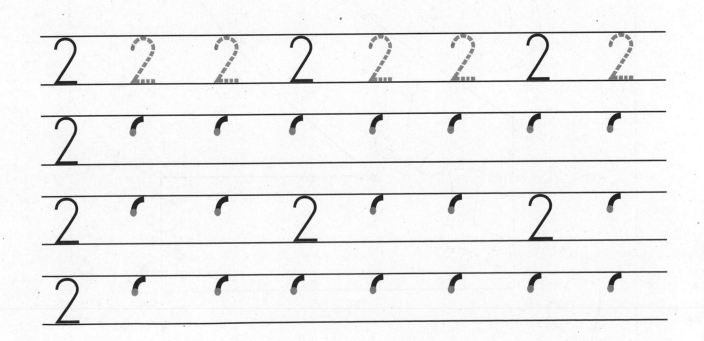

UNIT 1 LESSON 8

Scenes of 2, 3, and 4 **11**

Name _____

Going Further

What number is hiding in the picture?

Color spaces with 2 pictures red.

Color spaces with 1, 3, or 4 pictures yellow.

Scenes of 2, 3, and 4

Dear Family:

Your child is learning to write numbers. You might notice that sometimes your child might write numbers backwards or reverse them. This is very common in early number writing. You can ask your child, "Does this number look OK?" Then point out that it is written backwards. Eventually our goal is that children may identify their own reversals, write correct numbers, and write faster in preparation for first grade.

Thank you!

Sincerely,
Your child's teacher

Carta a la familia

Estimada familia:

Su niño está aprendiendo a escribir los números. Usted observará que a veces su niño escribe los números al revés o que los invierte. Esto es normal al empezar a escribir los números. Puede preguntarle, "¿Está bien escrito este número?" Luego indíquele que está escrito al revés. Nuestro objetivo es que los niños se den cuenta de que invierten los números, que los escriban correctamente y que escriban más rápido para prepararse para el primer grado.

¡Gracias!

Atentamente,
El maestro de su niño

Scenes of 2, 3, and 4

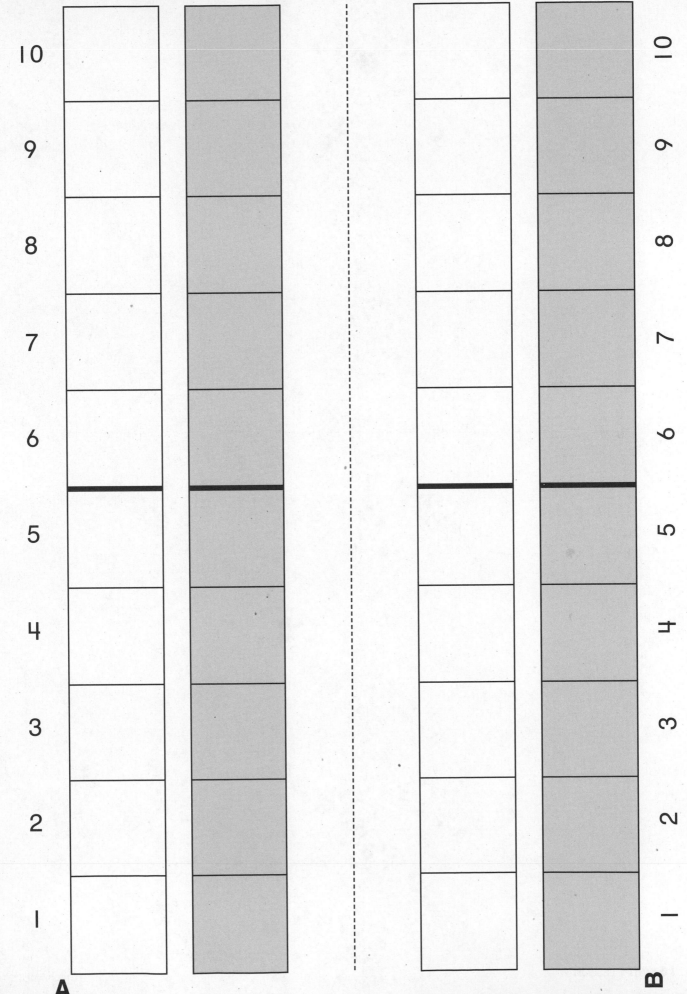

Graph Mat

Vocabulary
same
alike
different

Ring the pictures that are the **same**. They are **alike**.
Cross out the picture that is **different**. It is not like the other 2.

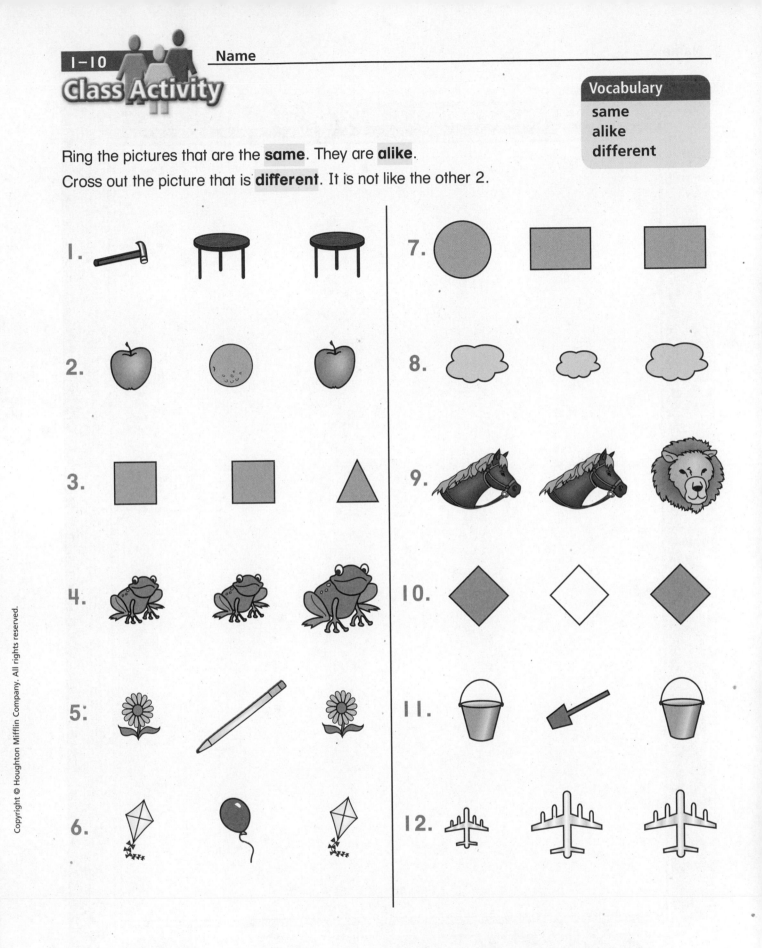

On the Back Draw 2 objects that are the same. Then draw another object that is different.

UNIT 1 LESSON 10

Scenes of 2, 3, 4, and 5 **17**

Scenes of 2, 3, 4, and 5

Class Activity

Name _____

Ring the pictures that are the same. They are alike.

Cross out the picture that is different. It is not like the other 2.

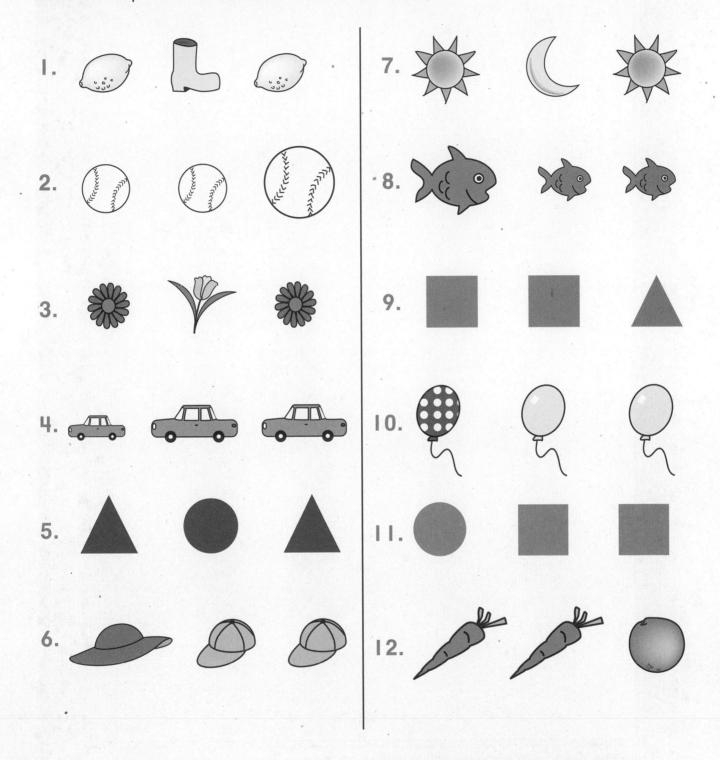

➡️ **On the Back** Draw 2 objects that are the same. Then draw another object that is different.

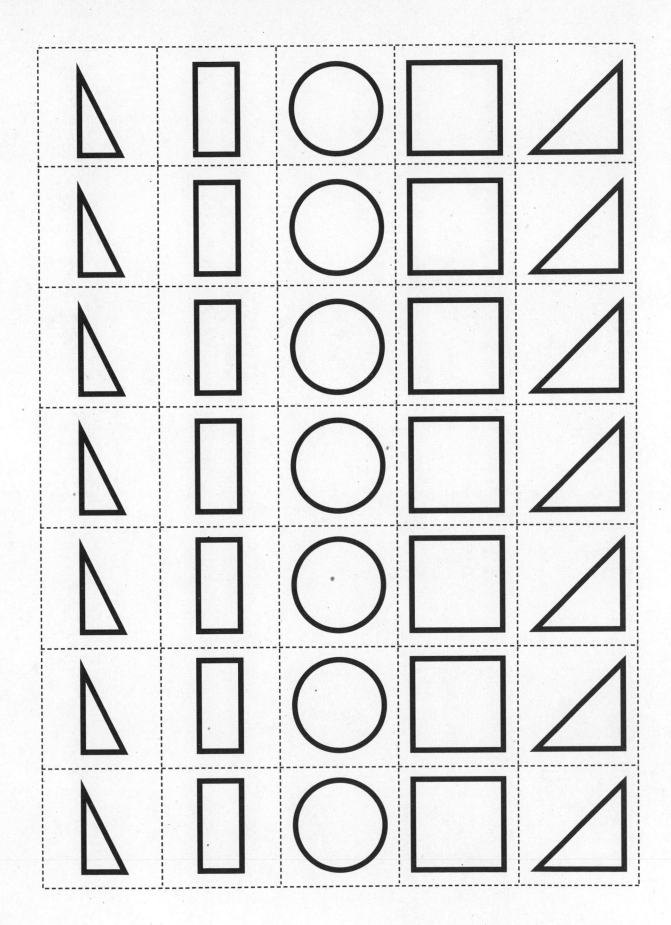

Shape Cards **21**

Shape Cards

Class Activity

Name _____

Write the number 3.

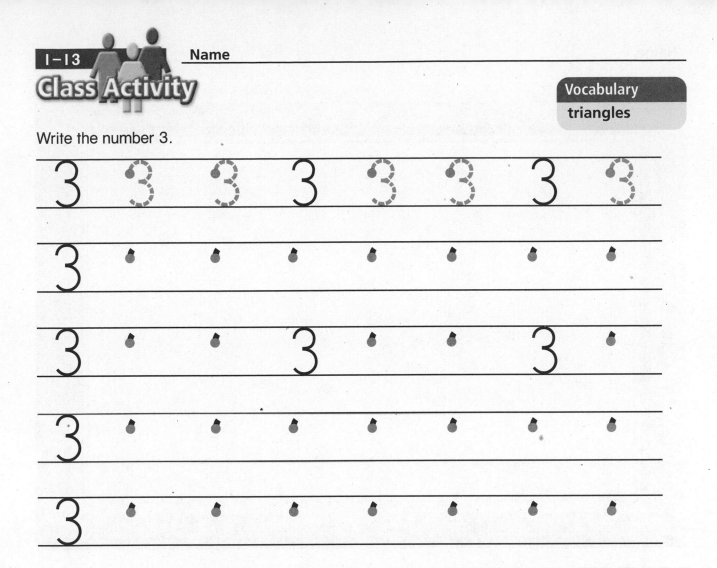

Draw 3 things.	Draw 3 **triangles** .

➡ **On the Back** Draw 3 animals. Then practice writing the numbers 1 and 2.

2 2 2 2 2 2 2

2 2 2 2 2 2 2

Exploration of Shapes

Class Activity

Name

Go left to right. Ring **groups** of the number. X out groups that are not the number.

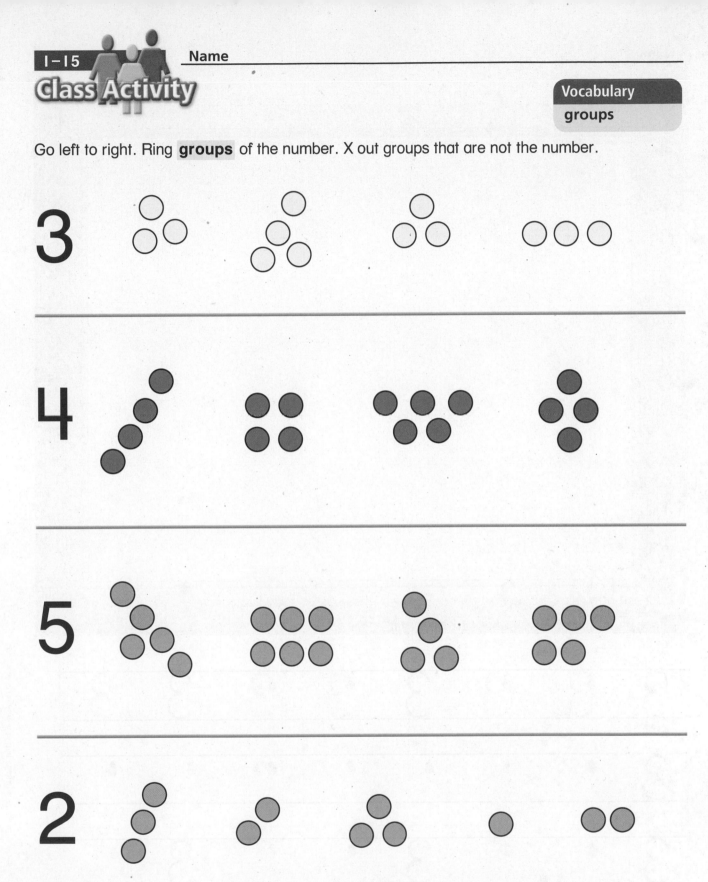

3

4

5

2

⮕ **On the Back** Draw a group of 3 circles. Then practice writing the number 3.

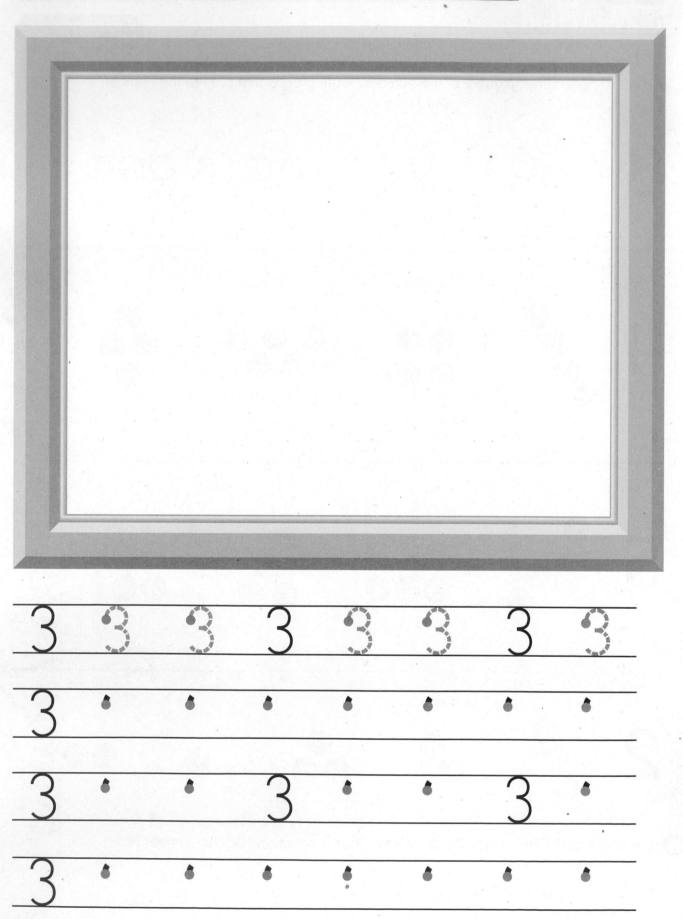

Number of Objects in a Group

Going Further

Vocabulary
circles
squares

Color the **circles** yellow. Color the **squares** blue.
Draw your face under your favorite hat.

➡ **On the Back** Draw 3 circles and 3 squares. Then practice writing the number 3.

2- and 3-Dimensional Shapes: Circle and Ball

Class Activity

Name _____

Paste shapes in each box to show that number.

1

2

3

Class Activity

Write the number 4.

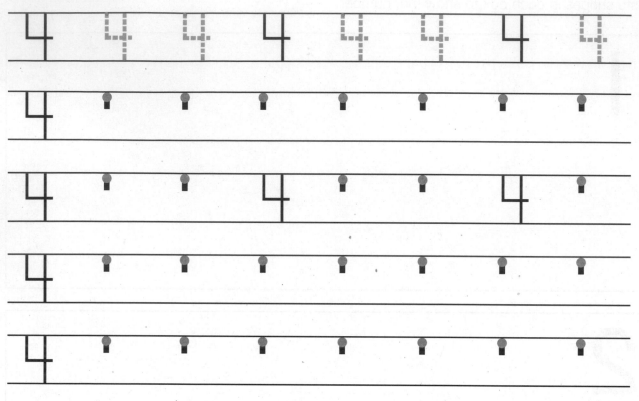

Draw 4 things.	Draw 4 triangles.

More Numbers of Objects in a Group

Name _____

Trace over the number 4. Color each group of 4 a different color.

Cross out the objects that are not in a group of 4.

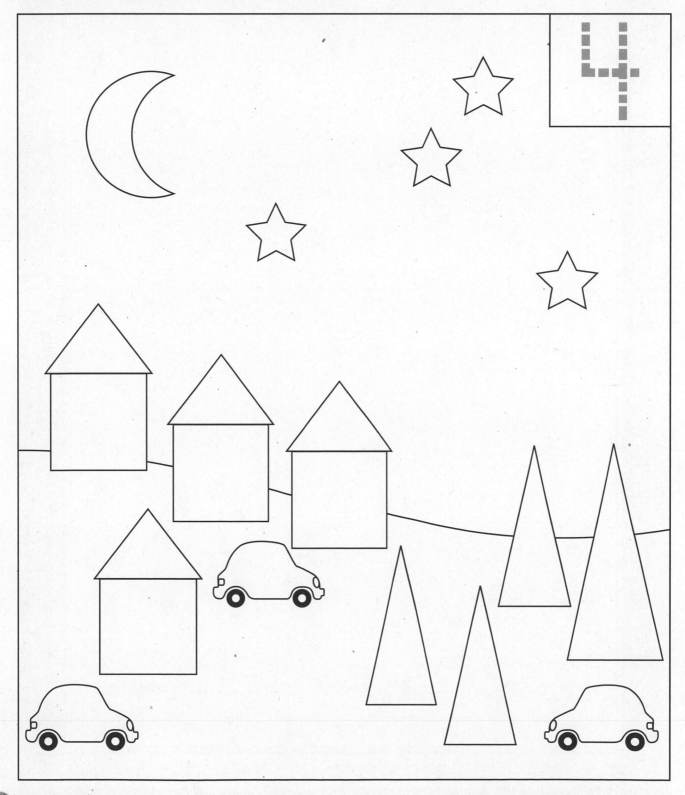

➡️ **On the Back** Draw a scene with 4 plates and 4 cups.

More Numbers of Objects in a Group

Name _____

Go left to right. Ring groups of the number. X out groups that are not the number.

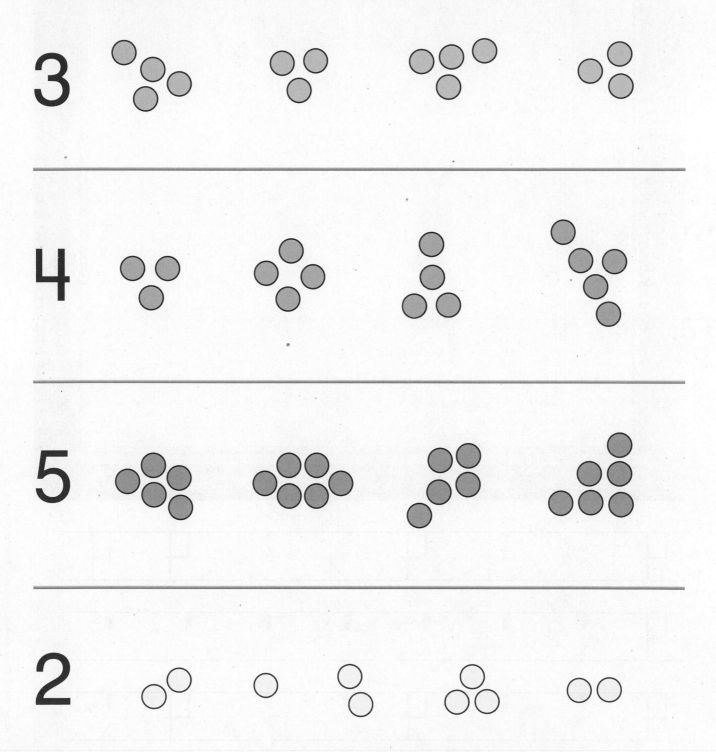

➡ **On the Back** Draw a group of 4 squares. Then practice writing the number 4.

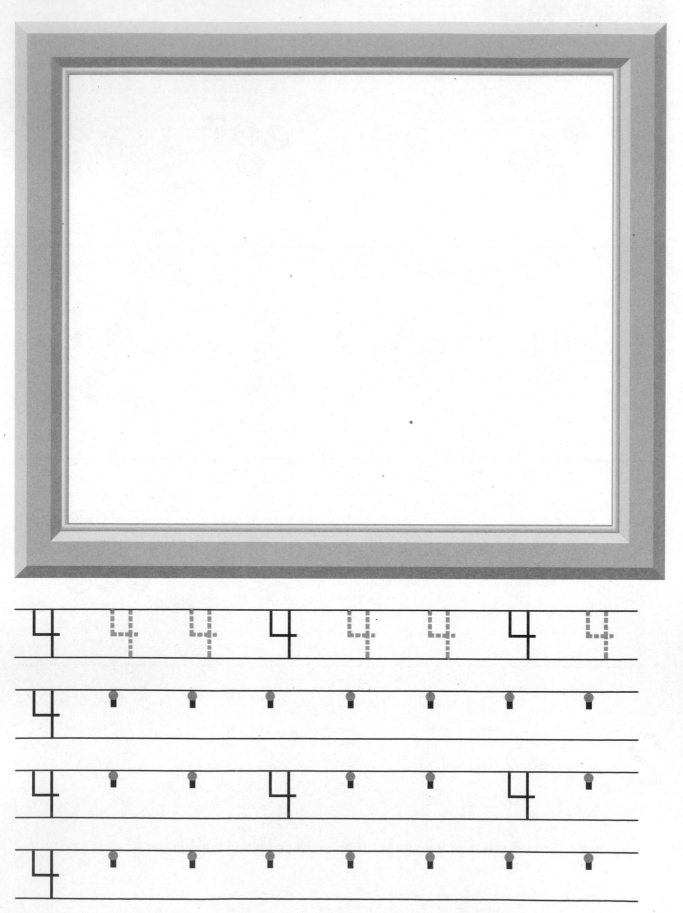

Objects and Numbers Through 10: Centimeter Cubes

Name _____

Paste shapes in each box to show that number.

4

5

Practice: Number of Objects in a Group **35**

Class Activity

Write the number 5.

5 5 5 5 5 5 5 5

5

5   5   5

5

5

Draw 5 things.

Draw 5 squares.

Practice: Number of Objects in a Group

Extra Practice

Count the animals. Ring the number. Then color each group a different color.

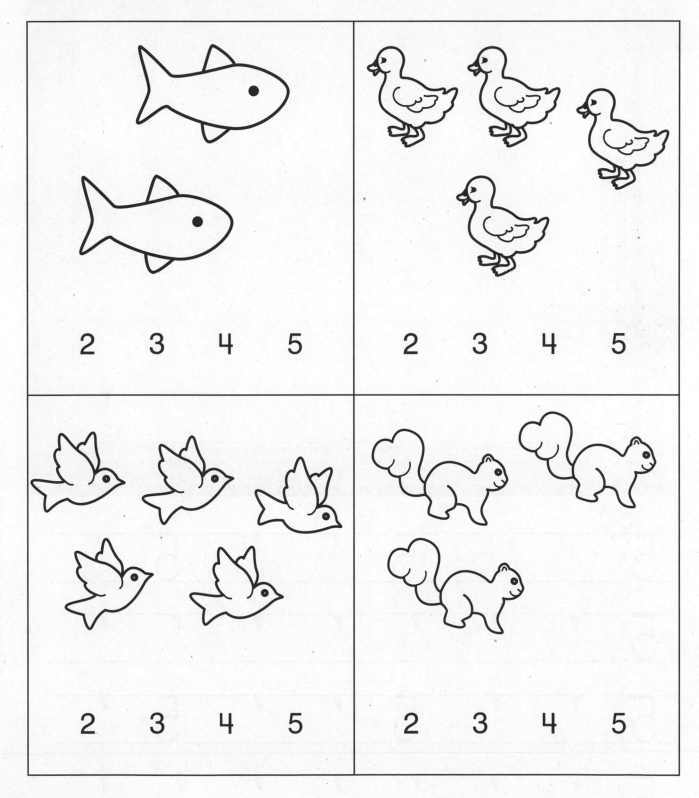

2   3   4   5

2   3   4   5

2   3   4   5

2   3   4   5

On the Back Draw 5 triangles. Then practice writing the number 5.

5 5 5 5 5 5 5

5

5 5 5

5

Practice: Number of Objects in a Group

Name _____

Class Activity

Connect the dots in **order**.

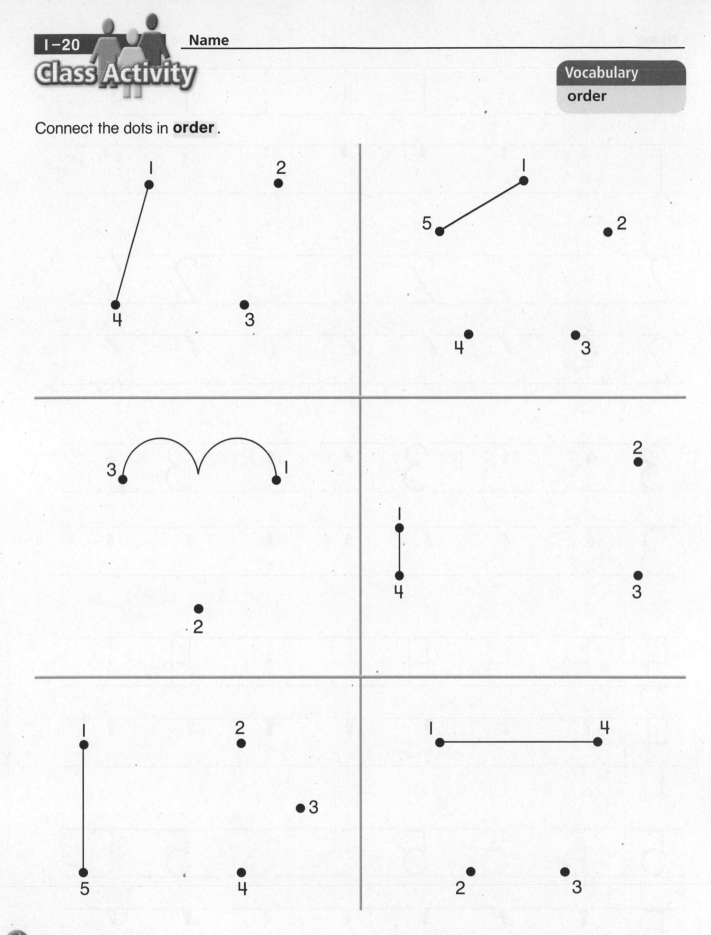

→ **On the Back** Practice writing the numbers 1, 2, 3, 4, and 5.

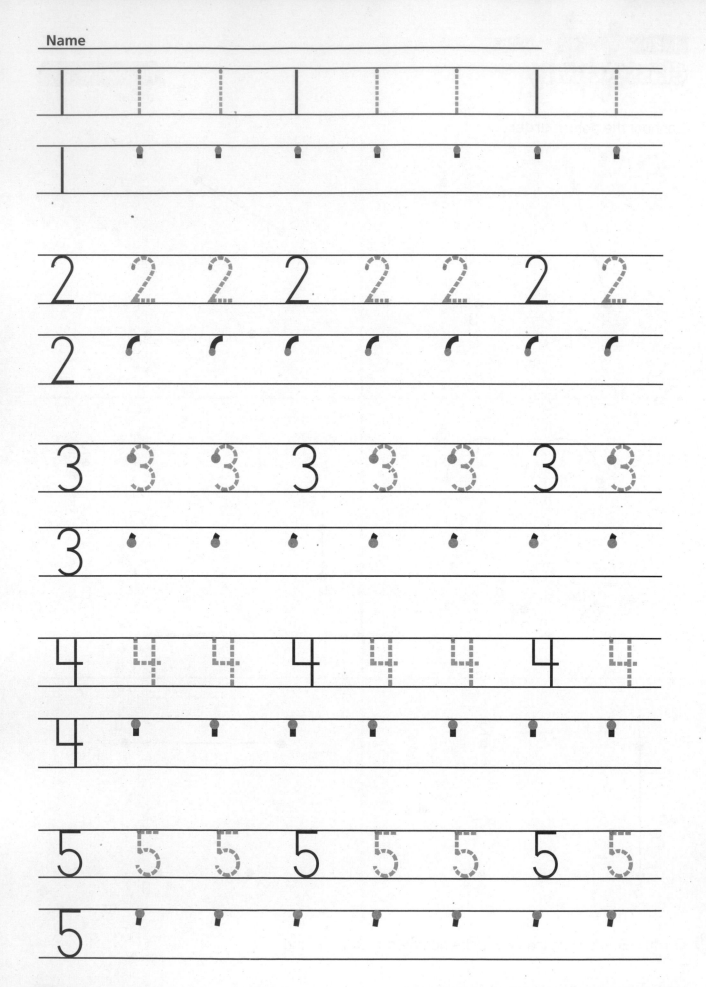

More Objects and Numbers Through 10: Square-Inch Tiles

Class Activity

Connect the dots in order.

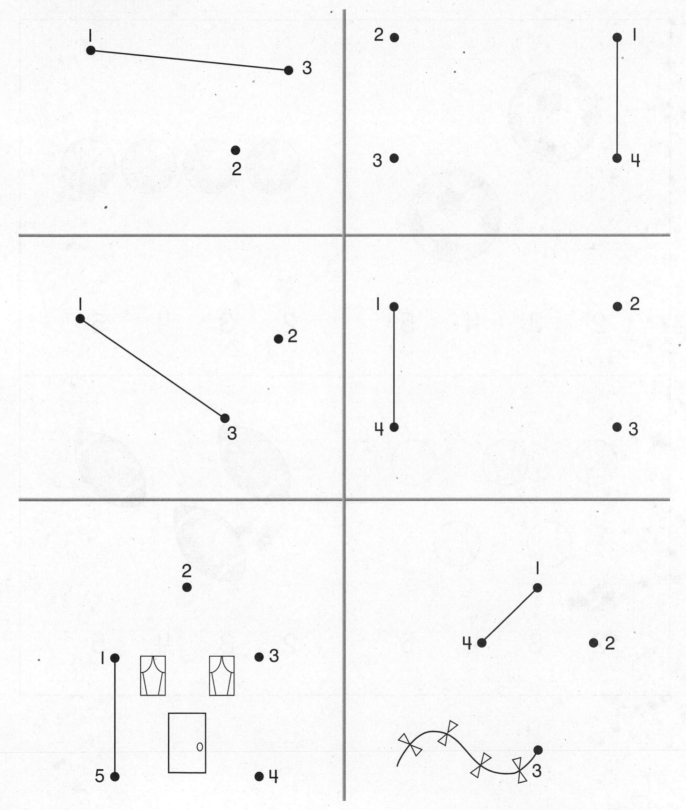

More Scenes of 2, 3, 4, and 5 **41**

Count the balls. Ring the number.

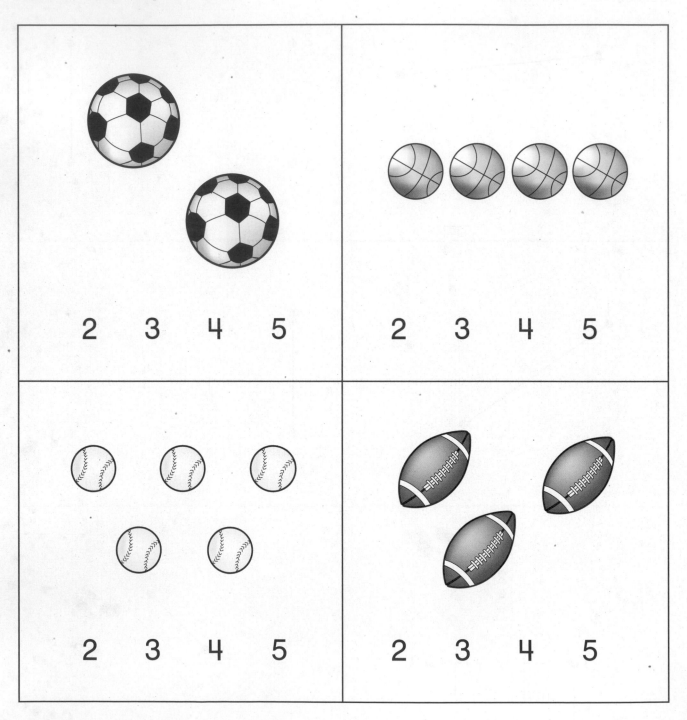

More Scenes of 2, 3, 4, and 5

Extra Practice

Read the number. Look for that number of things in your classroom.

Draw the group of things that matches the number.

3	2

5

4

➡ **On the Back** Practice writing the numbers 1, 2, 3, 4, and 5.

Name

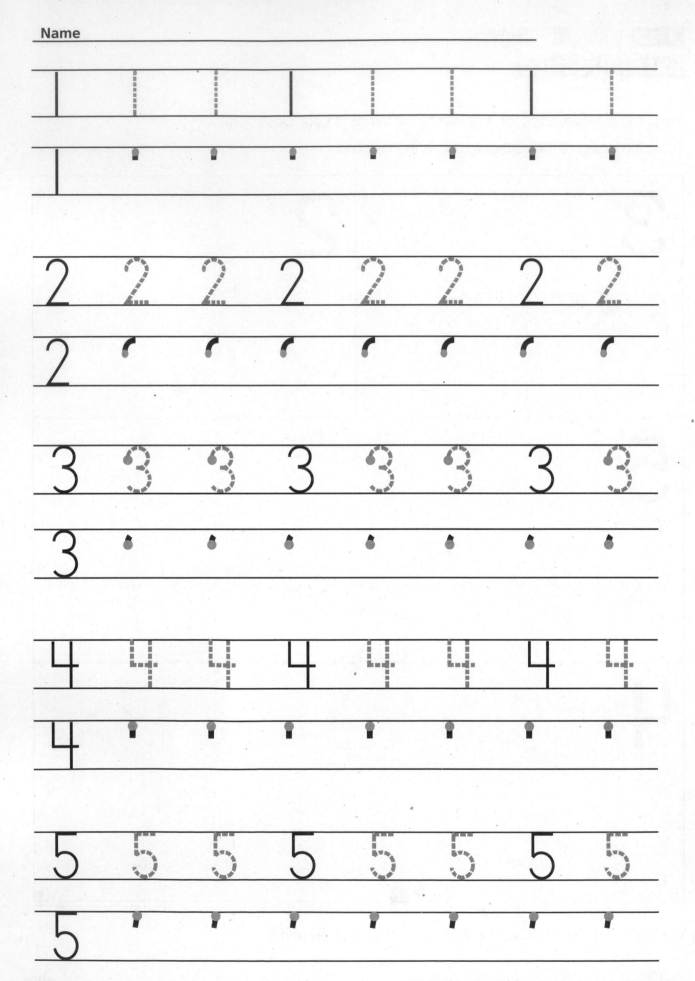

More Objects and Numbers Through 10: Centimeter Cubes

Going Further

Name _____

Connect the shoes that make a **pair**. Ring the shoe that is not part of a pair.

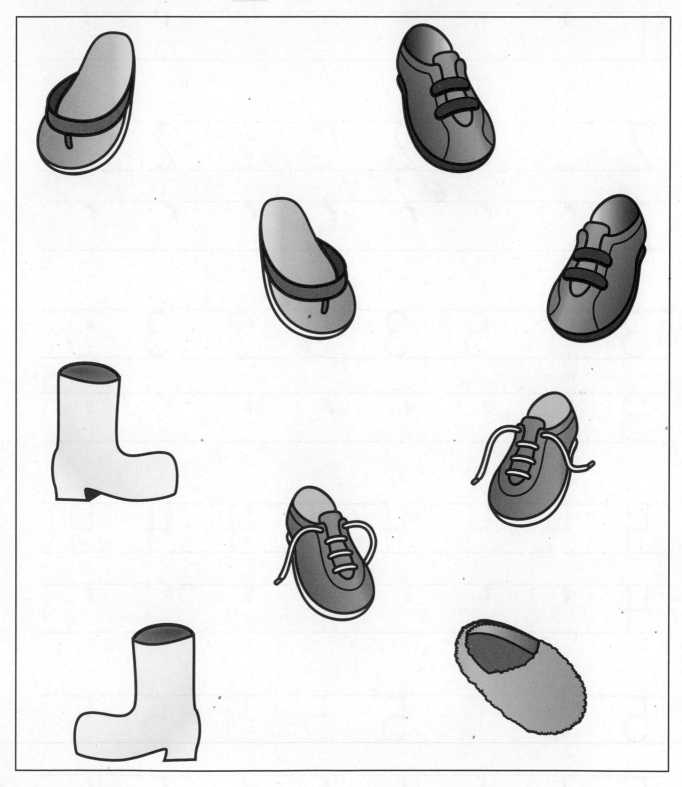

➡ **On the Back** Practice writing the numbers 1, 2, 3, 4, and 5.

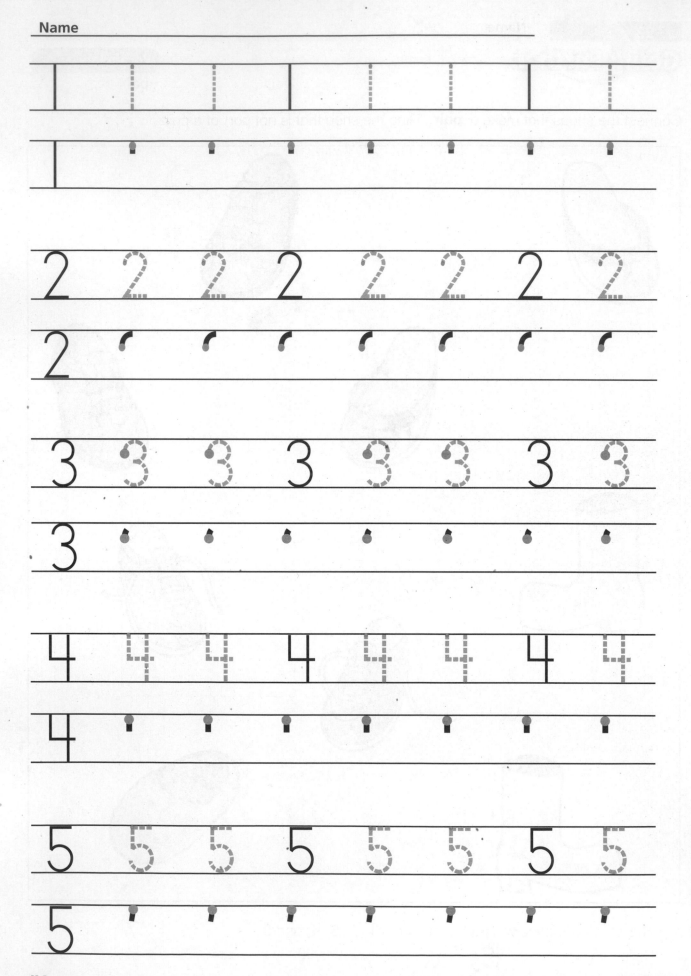

Scenes of I

Color all the shapes of one kind the same color.

Count the number of each shape in the picture. Write the number.

● [3] red

■ [ ] blue

◆ [ ] green

▰ [ ] purple

▲◗ [ ] orange

▮ [ ] yellow

Name _____

Ring the group of shapes you could use to make the tower.

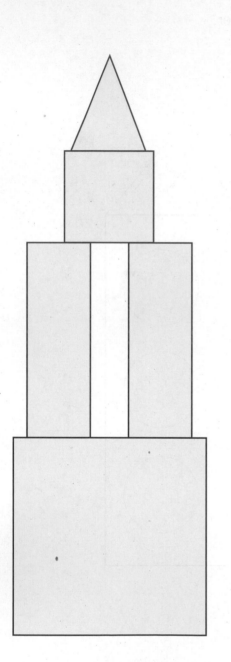

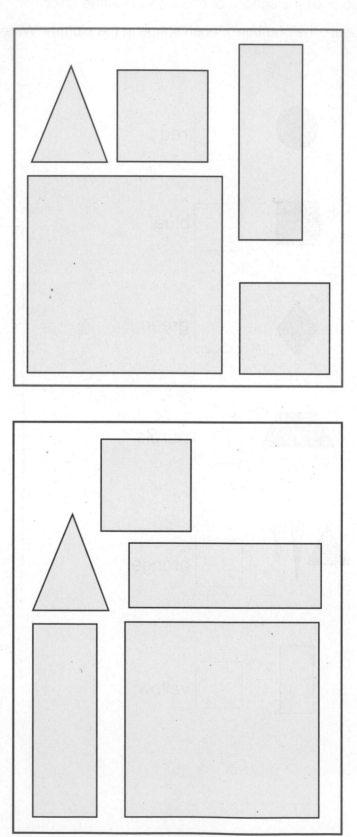

Make a Class Graph

Name _____

Move along the paths.

1. Start on the pond.

Go to the bench.

Show how you moved.

2. Start at the swings.

Go to the tunnel.

Show how you moved.

3. Start at the flower garden.

Go to the swings.

Show how you moved.

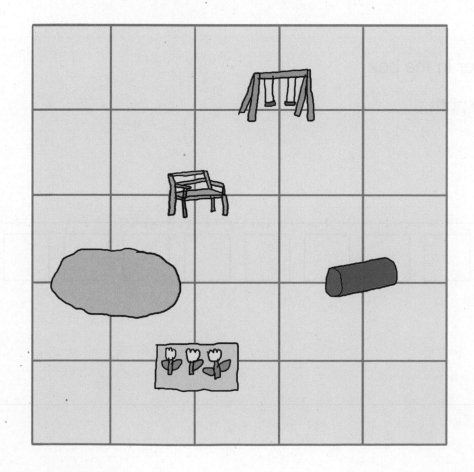

Name _____

Help the frog hop.

Write each hop number in the box.

Stop at the end of the path.

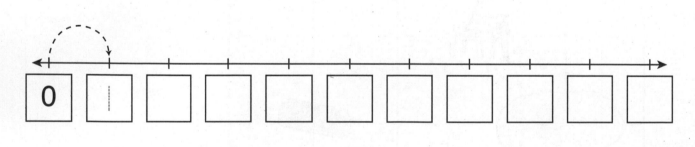

Use Mathematical Processes

Name _____

Exercises 1–2. Ring the groups of the number. X out groups that are not the number.

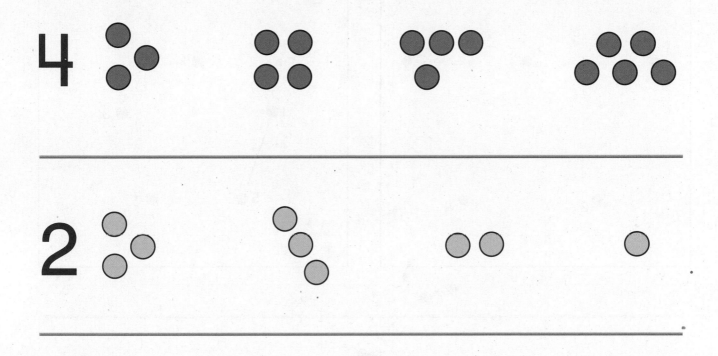

Exercises 3–4. Draw.

Draw 3 circles.	Draw 5 triangles.

Exercises 5–6. Connect the dots in order.

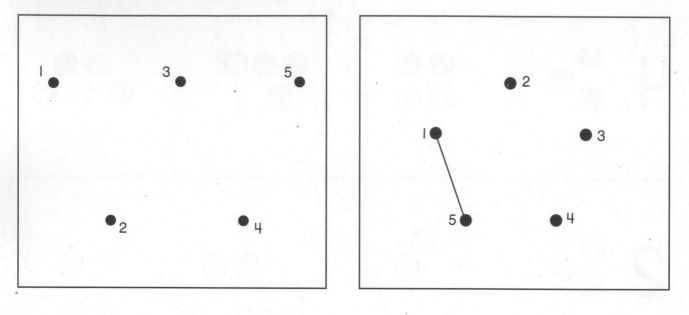

Exercises 7–8.

Ring the pictures that are the **same**. They are **alike**.

Cross out the object that is **different**. It is not like the other 2.

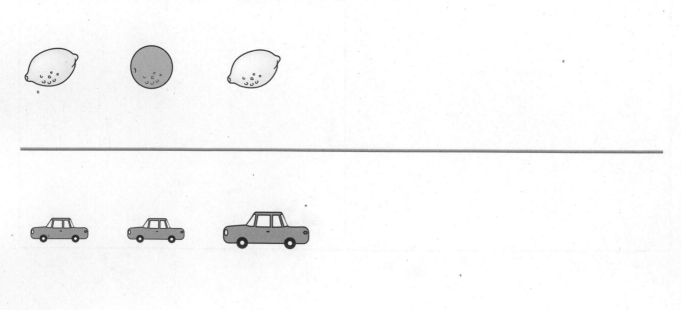

Exercise 9. Write the numbers.

Exercise 10. **Extended Response** Make a drawing. Use 1 circle, 2 triangles, 3 squares, and 4 lines.

Name _____

Find groups of 1 through 10.

On the Back Draw 8 bugs. Show a 5-group and extras.

Find Numbers 1–10: Neighborhood Scene

Dear Family:

Children are learning to see numbers 6, 7, 8, 9, and 10 as having a 5 and some more. This is called using a 5-group. This visual pattern will help children add, subtract, and understand numbers. It will also help later in multidigit calculation.

Count things at home in 5-groups to help your child see the 5 in 6, 7, 8, 9, and 10. For example, 7 buttons can be counted using 5-groups: "5 and 2 make 7."

Children will see 5-groups in materials they are using in school:

Number Parade

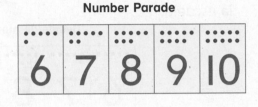

Square-Inch Tiles

6 7 8 9 10

Pennies and Nickel Strips

6 7 8 9 10

Thank you!

Sincerely,
Your child's teacher

Please send 20 pennies to school with your child. Pennies will be used with Nickel Strips to show numbers.

Estimada familia:

Los niños están aprendiendo a ver que los números 6, 7, 8, 9 y 10 contienen el 5 y algo más. Esto se llama usar un grupo de 5. Este patrón visual los ayudará a sumar, a restar y a entender los números. Más adelante también les servirá para los cálculos con números de más de un dígito.

Cuenten cosas en casa haciendo grupos de 5 para que el niño identifique el 5 en el 6, 7, 8, 9 y 10. Por ejemplo, pueden contar 7 botones haciendo un grupo de 5: "5 más 2 son 7".

Los niños identificarán grupos de 5 en los materiales que usan en la escuela:

Desfile de números

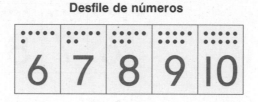

Azulejos de una pulgada cuadrada

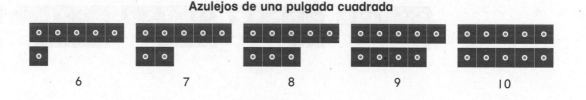

Monedas de un centavo y tiras de cinco centavos

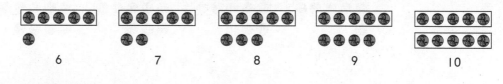

Muchas gracias.

Atentamente,
El maestro de su niño

Por favor, envíe 20 monedas de un centavo a la escuela con su niño. Las usaremos con las tiras de monedas de cinco centavos para mostrar los números.

Find Numbers 1–10: Neighborhood Scene

Cut on dashed lines.
Do not cut on solid lines.

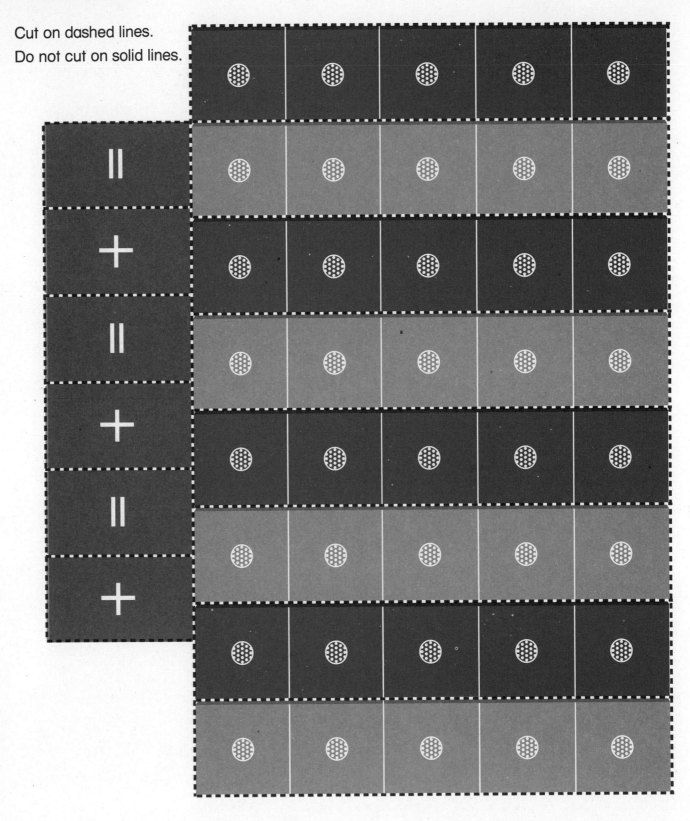

5-Square Tiles **59**

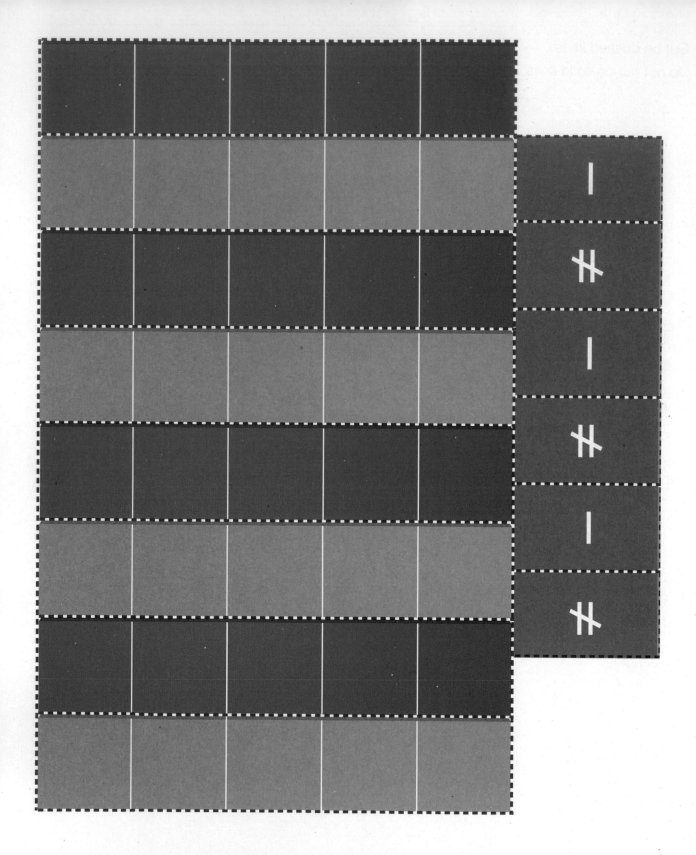

5-Square Tiles

Name _____

Class Activity

Ring groups of the number. X out groups that are not the number.

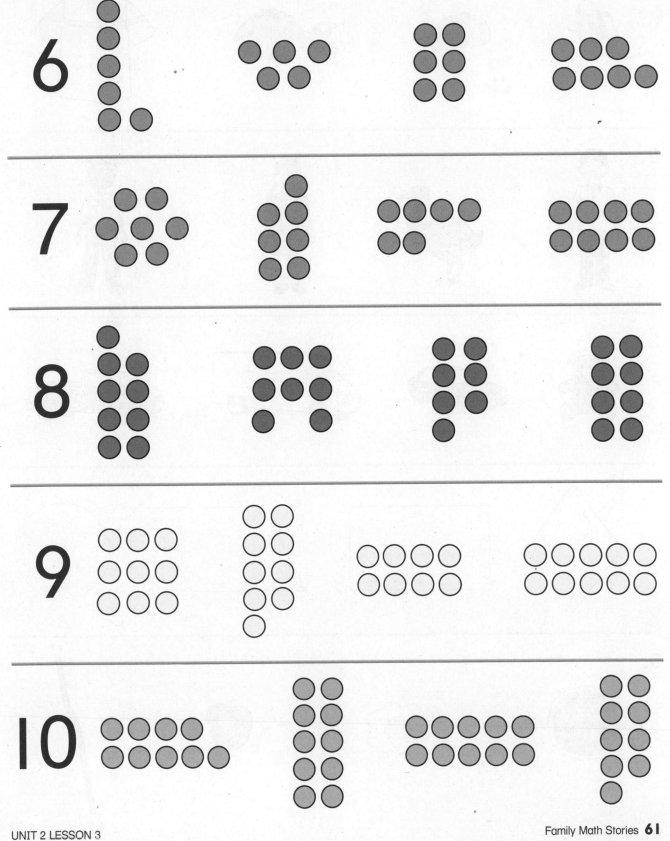

Family Math Stories **61**

Going Further

Name _____

X out the object in each row that does not belong.

1.

2.

3.

4.

5.

Family Math Stories

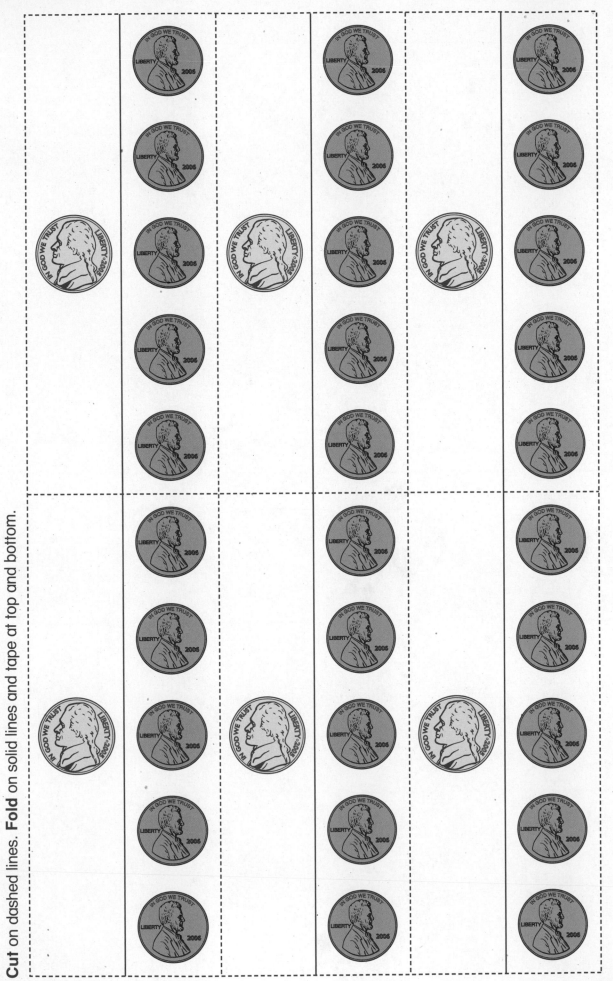

Cut on dashed lines. **Fold** on solid lines and tape at top and bottom.

Nickel Strips

Write the number 6.

6 6 6 6 6 6 6 6

6

6   6   6

6

Draw 6 things.	Draw 6 triangles.

On the Back Draw 6 fish. Then practice writing the number 6.

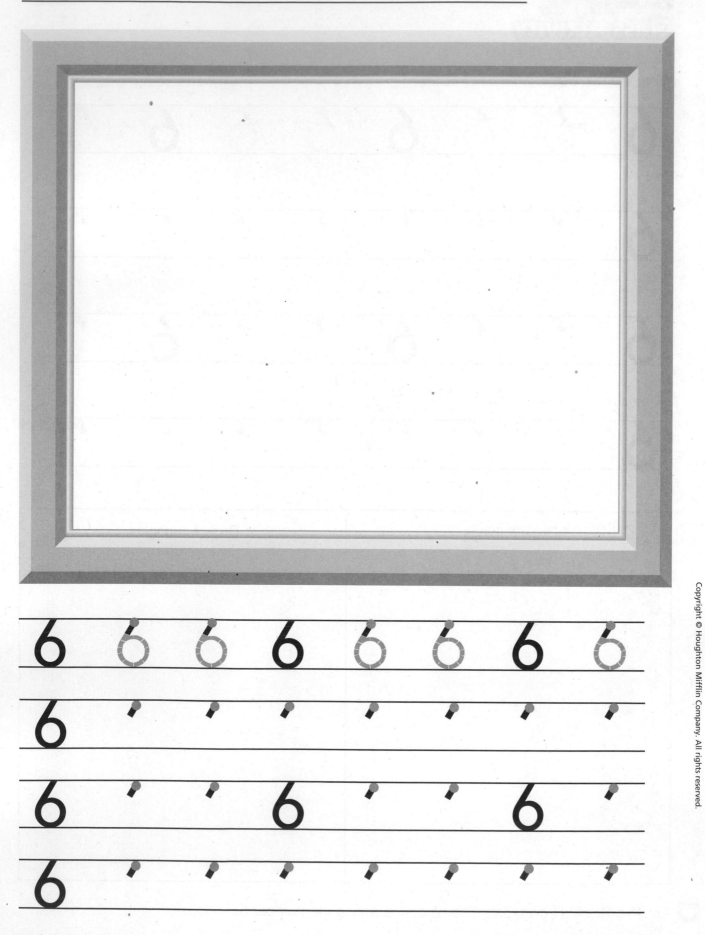

More Family Math Stories

Class Activity

Name _____

Continue the **patterns**.

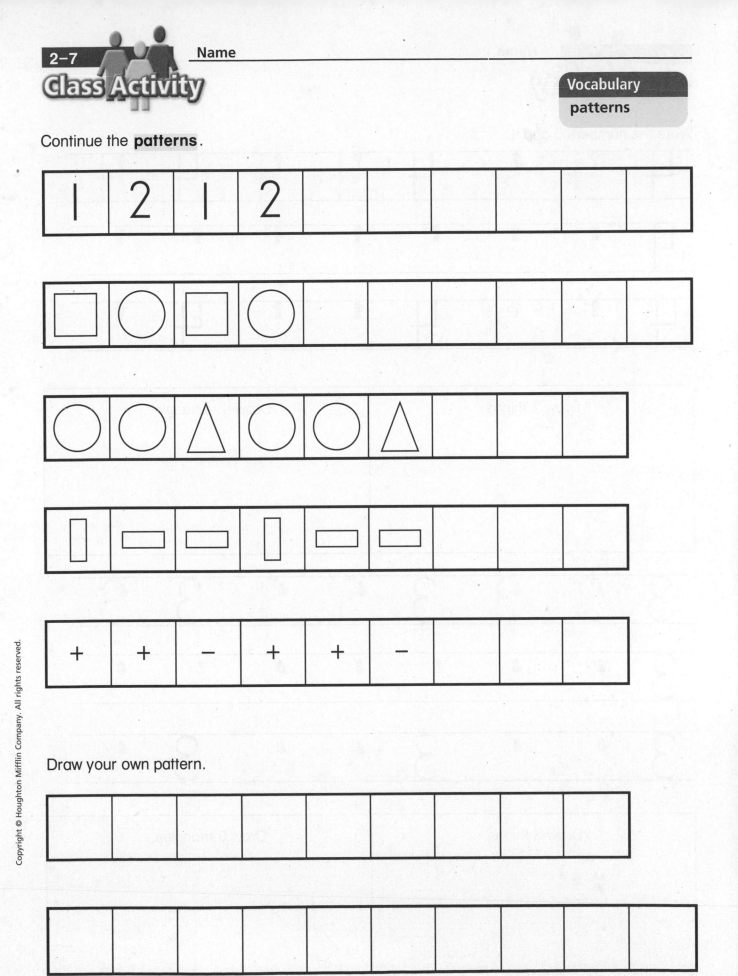

Draw your own pattern.

Make Repeating Patterns **67**

Write the numbers 3 and 4.

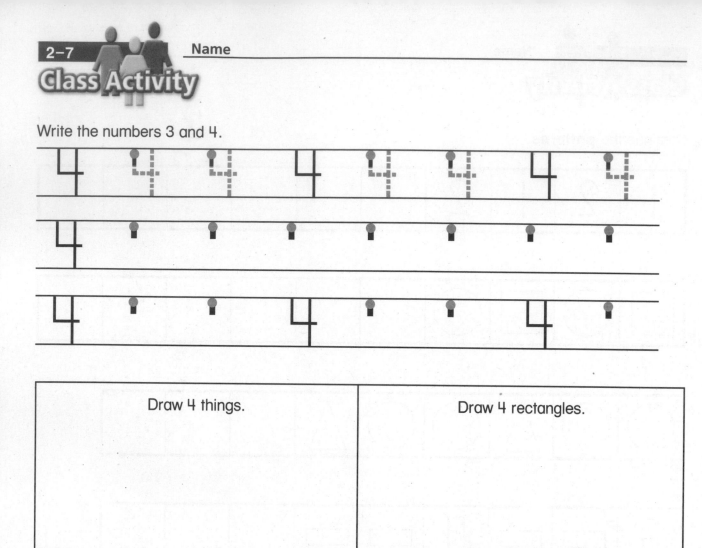

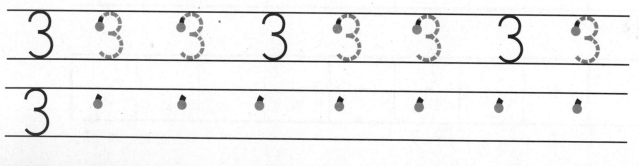

Draw 4 things.	Draw 4 rectangles.

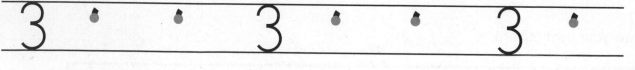

Draw 3 things.	Draw 3 triangles.

Make Repeating Patterns

Class Activity

Tell a math story.

Make a drawing to show how many balloons in all.

Addition and Subtraction Stories: Playground Scenario **69**

Class Activity

Name _____

Connect the dots in order. Use parts of **straight lines** .

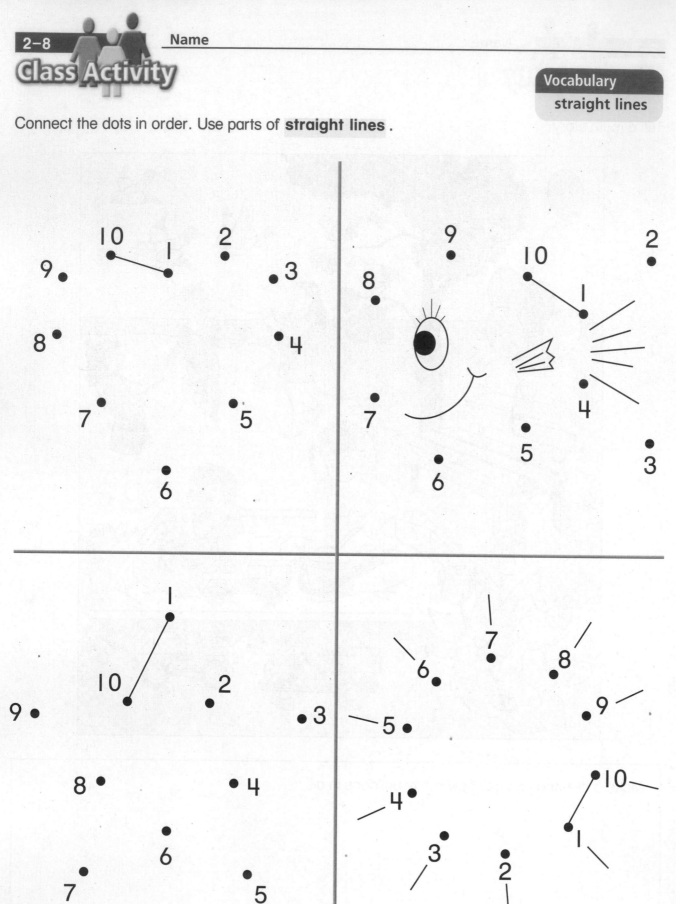

Addition and Subtraction Stories: Playground Scenario

+/− Tiles, =/≠ Tiles **71**

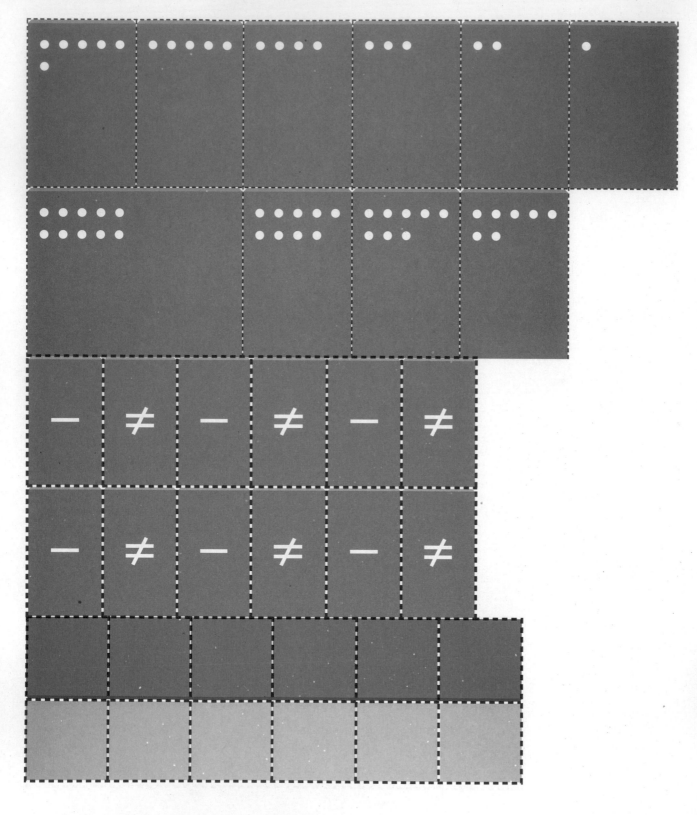

+/− Tiles, =/≠ Tiles

Class Activity

Name _____

Write the numbers 2 and 5.

Draw 2 things.	Draw 2 circles.

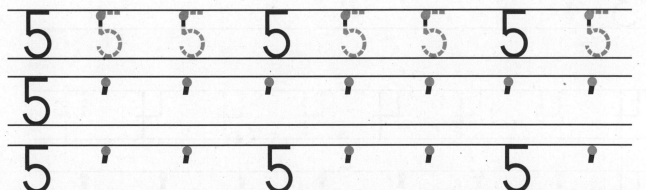

Draw 5 things.	Draw 5 squares.

On the Back Write numbers 1–5 in order. Use the Number Parade to help.

More Coin Values and Numbers 6–10 **73**

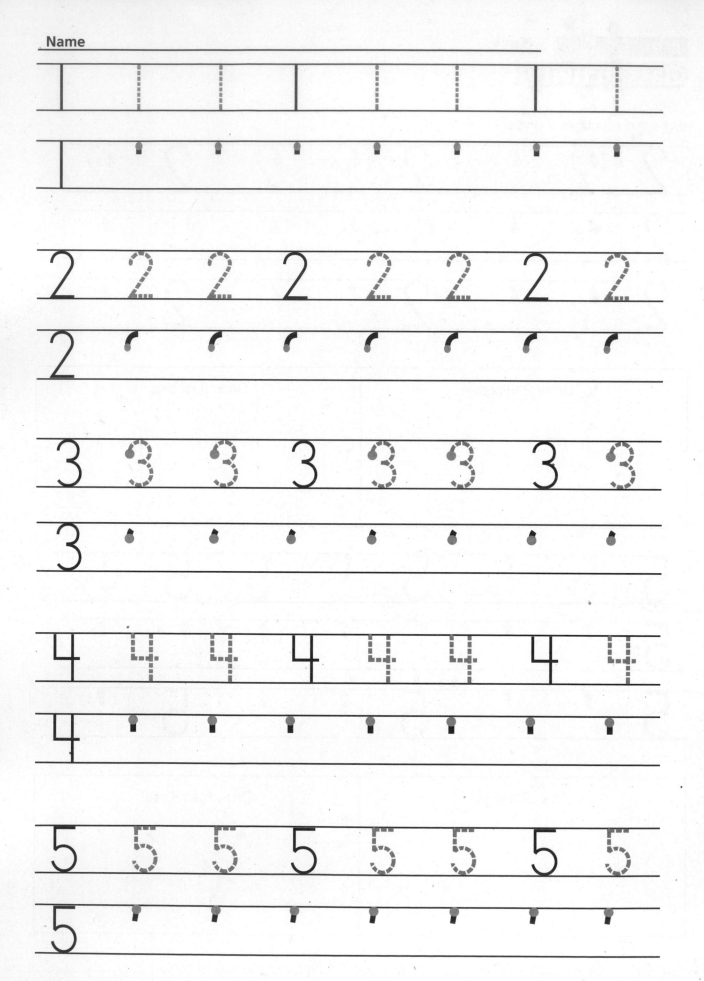

More Coin Values and Numbers 6–10

Write the number 7.

Draw 7 things.

Draw 7 squares.

Class Activity

Name _____

Connect the dots in order.

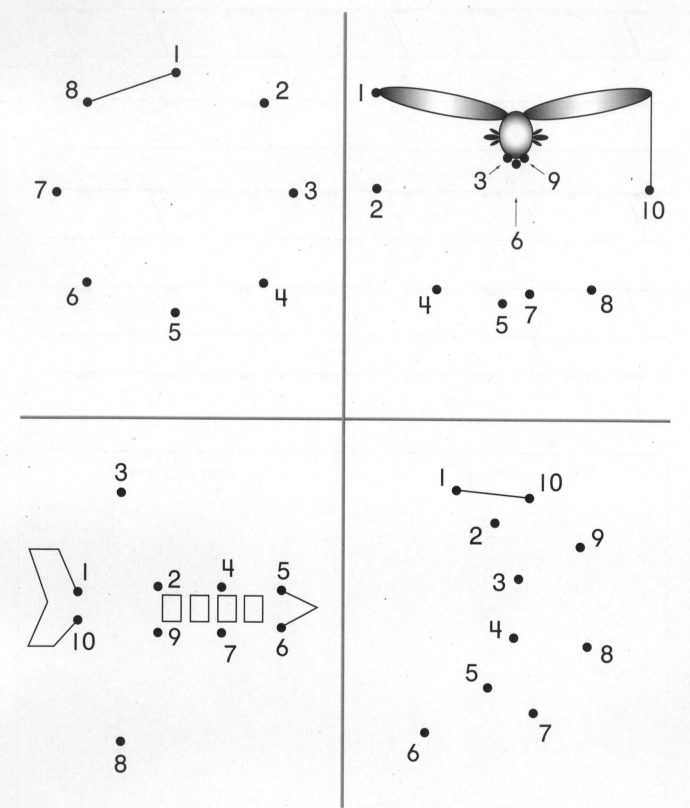

2- and 3-Dimensional Shapes: Rectangles and Boxes

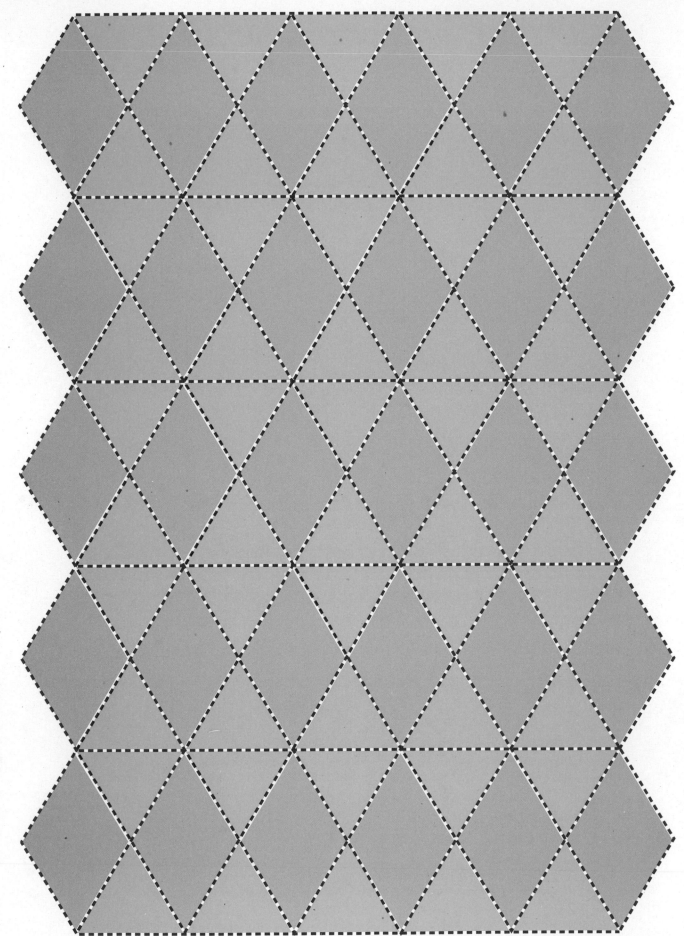

Pattern Blocks: Triangles and Parallelograms **77**

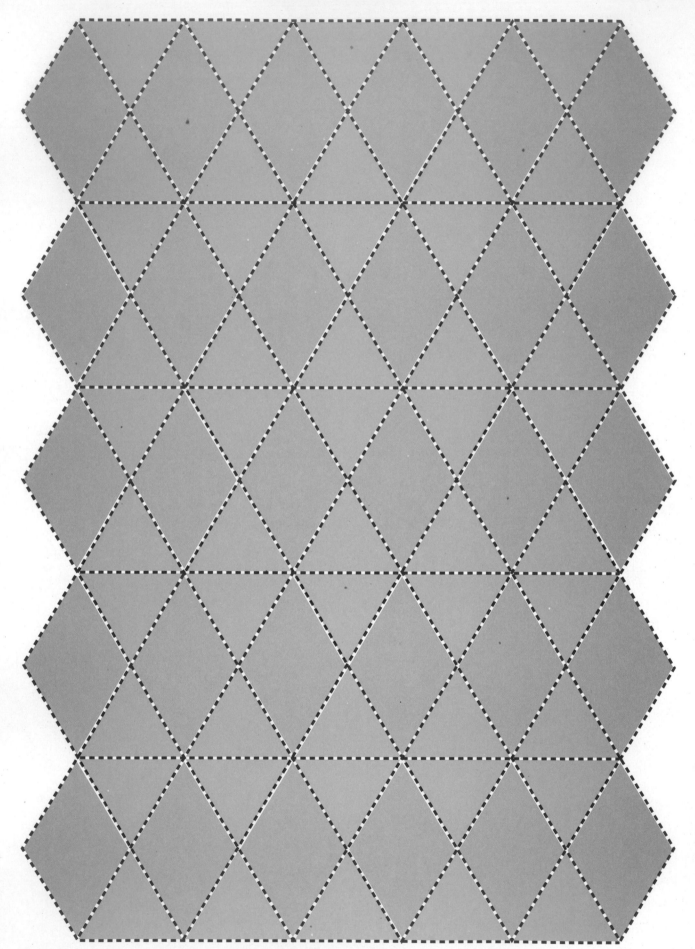

Pattern Blocks: Triangles and Parallelograms

Class Activity

Name

Use a pencil or marker and trace each number 2 times. Use the color blue to trace the 6s and the color red to trace the 7s.

Write the numbers 1 to 7.

➡ **On the Back** Write the numbers 1 to 7 in different sizes.

Practice with 5-Groups

Name _____

Discuss shapes you see. Then trace the shapes and draw them below the pictures.

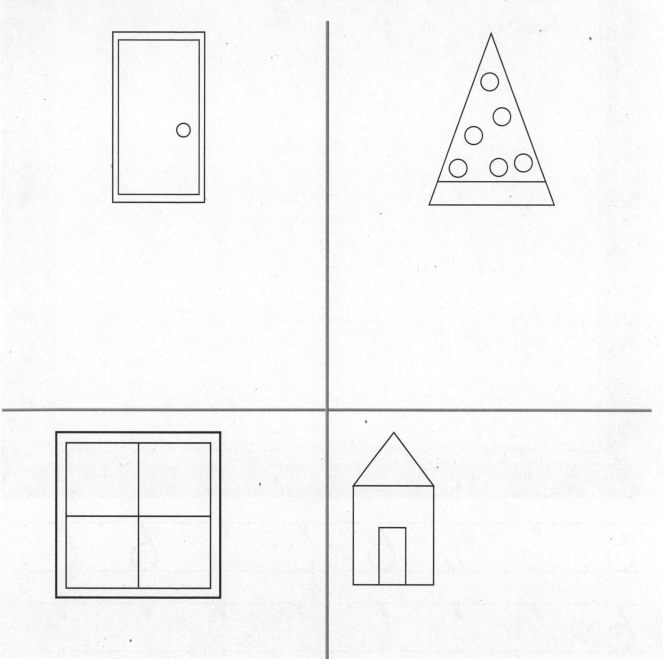

On the Back Use shapes to draw a birdhouse. Then practice writing the number 6.

Investigate Shapes in Our World

Dear Family:

Children in our class are discovering and finding shapes in their world. They are examining the shapes of books, windows, wheels, televisions, coins, traffic signs, and so on. You can help your child learn by asking what shapes he or she can see and name in and around your home. Your child can practice drawing different shapes, too!

Look below to see some of the many different kinds of shapes our class will explore this school year:

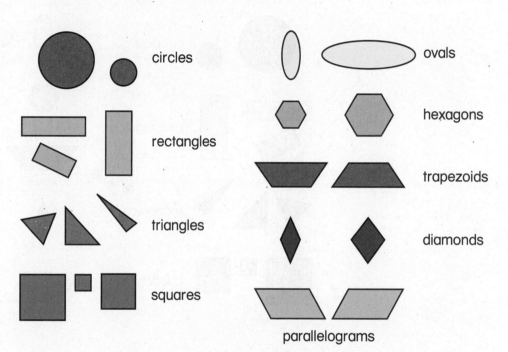

We would love to hear about shapes your child has discovered at home. Tell your child to share them with us at school!

Thank you.

Sincerely,
Your child's teacher

Carta a la familia

Estimada familia:

Los niños de nuestra clase están descubriendo y hallando figuras en su mundo. Están examinando las figuras de los libros, las ventanas, las ruedas, los televisores, las monedas y las señales de tráfico. Usted puede ayudar a su niño a aprender preguntándole qué figuras puede ver e identificar dentro y fuera de la casa. ¡Su niño también puede practicar al dibujar las figuras!

A continuación se pueden ver algunos de los diferentes tipos de figuras que exploraremos en la clase durante este año escolar:

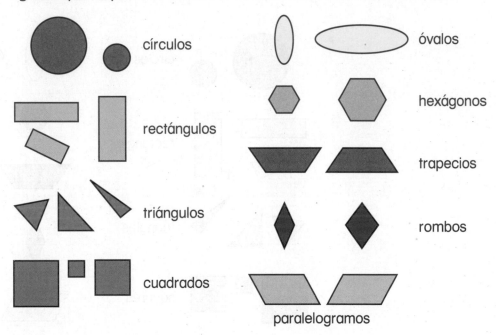

Nos encantaría saber qué figuras ha descubierto en casa su niño. ¡Dígale que comparta la información con nosotros en la escuela!

Muchas gracias.

Atentamente,
El maestro de su niño

Investigate Shapes in Our World

Class Activity

Name _____

Write the number 8.

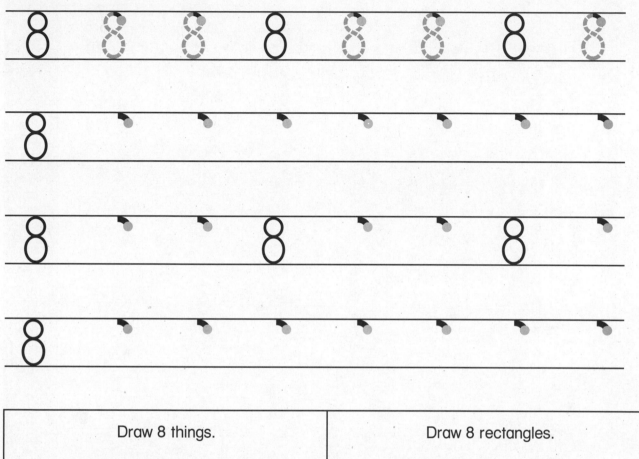

Draw 8 things.	Draw 8 rectangles.

➡ **On the Back** Draw 8 birds. Then practice writing the number 8.

Explore Number Patterns

Rectangles and Squares **87**

Introduce Number and Counting Routines

Name _____

Going Further

Vocabulary

more

Look at these beads:

5

Ring the groups that have **more** than 5 beads. Don't count.

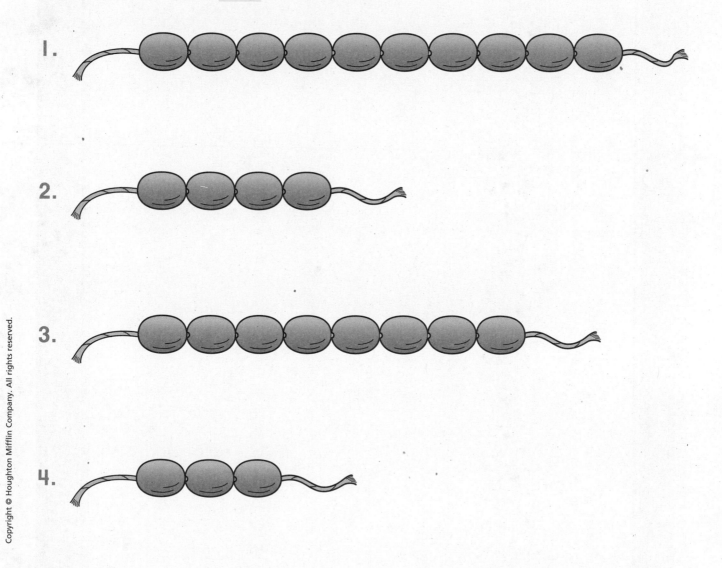

1.

2.

3.

4.

On the Back Draw some circles. Did you draw more than 5, exactly 5, or less than 5?

Numbers 1 Through 10

Tell a math story.

Addition and Subtraction Stories: Garden Scenario **91**

Class Activity

Name _____

Write the number 9.

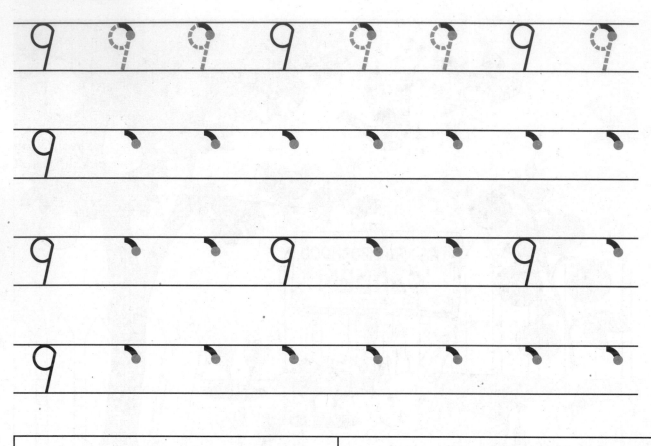

Draw 9 things.	Draw 9 triangles.

Addition and Subtraction Stories: Garden Scenario

Name _____

Going Further

Listen to the teacher. Ring Mio's ball.

Listen to the teacher. Draw Brad's ball.

On the Back Draw your own patterns. Then practice writing the number 9.

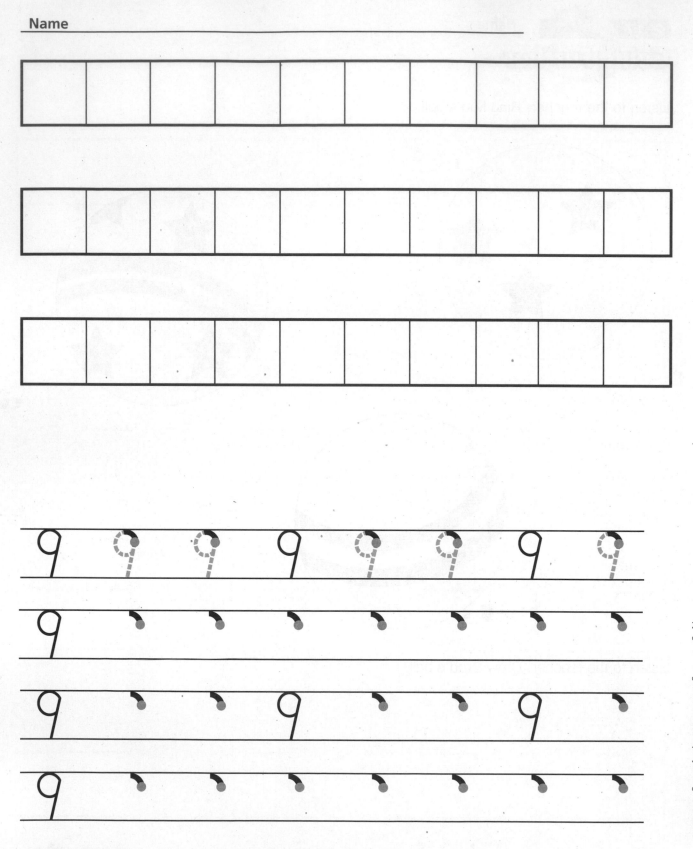

Numbers 1 Through 10: the +1 Pattern

Class Activity

Name _____

Vocabulary
pattern

Continue the **pattern** .

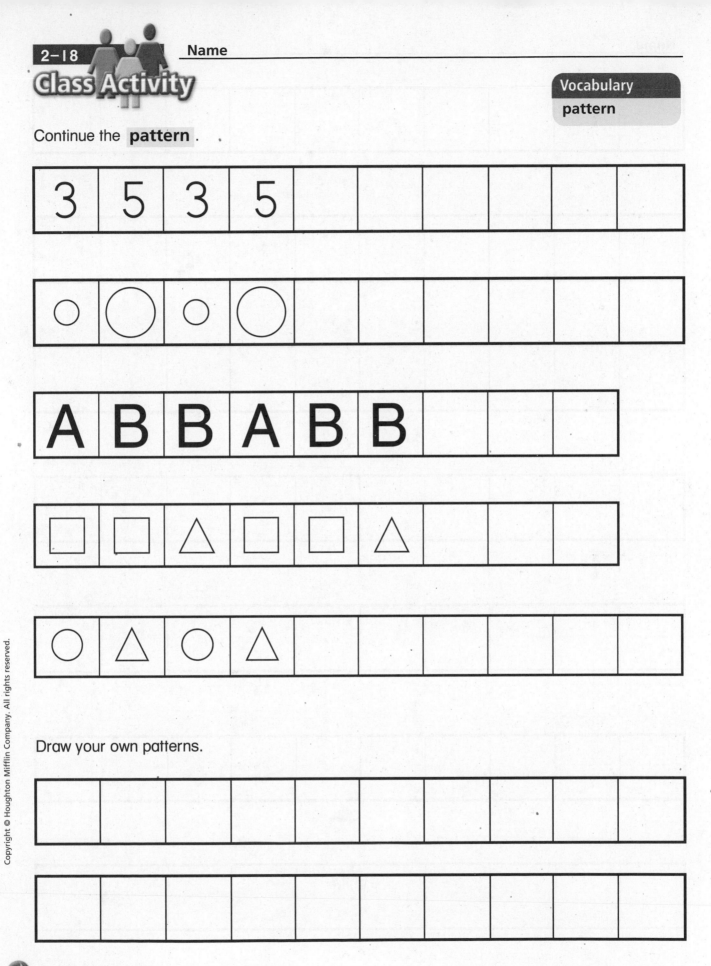

| 3 | 5 | 3 | 5 | | | | | |

Draw your own patterns.

➡ **On the Back** Draw your own patterns.

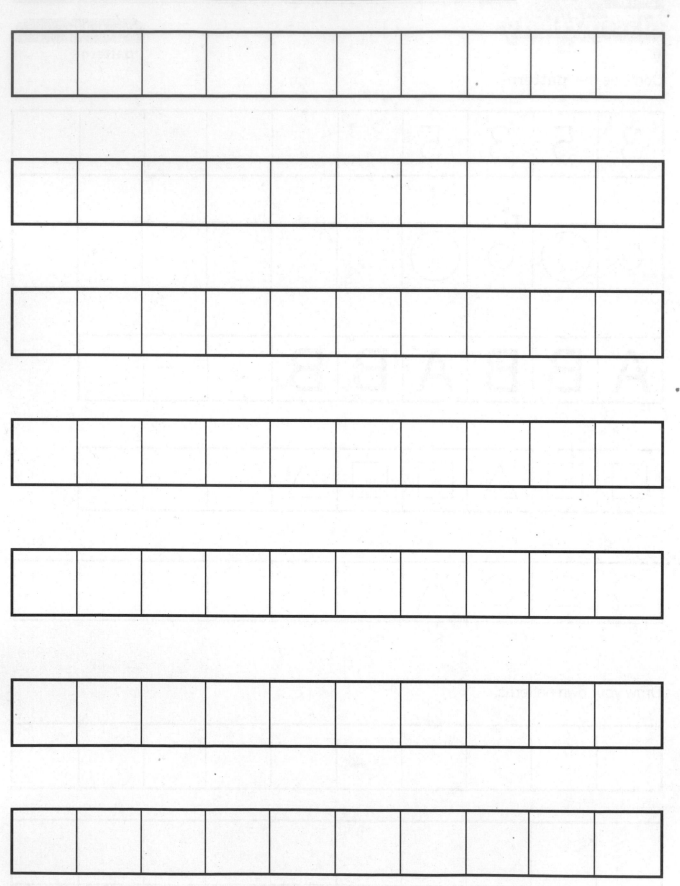

Find and Make New Patterns

Name _____

Going Further

Vocabulary
growing pattern

Continue each **growing pattern** .

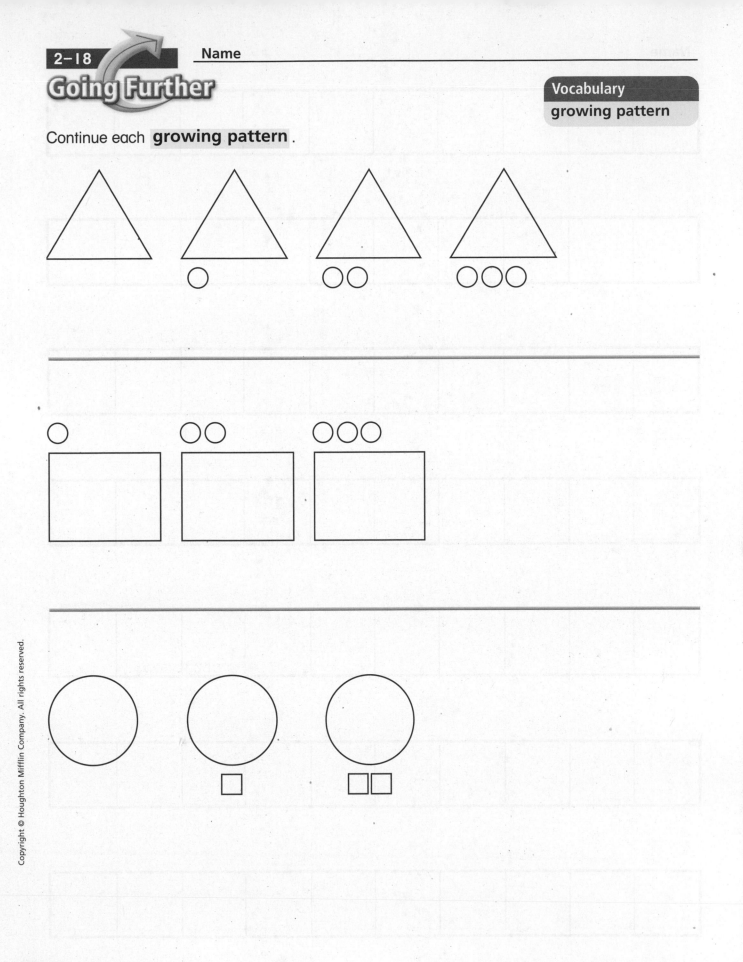

➡ **On the Back** Draw your own patterns.

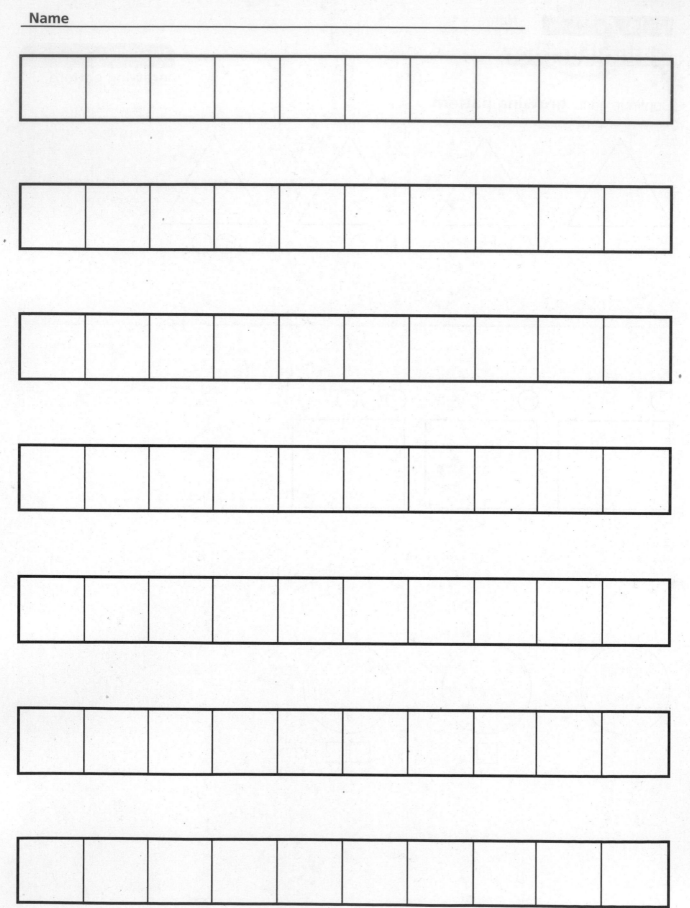

Find and Make New Patterns

Dear Family:

Your child is beginning to see and explore patterns they find in the world around them. Patterns are repeating objects, shapes, symbols, sounds, or body motions arranged over and over again in the same order.

Your child is learning about simple patterns. These will develop and become more complex as the year progresses. Children observe or make a pattern by reading or saying the pattern, moving from left to right.

You can help your child develop this concept by making some patterns at home, for example:

Patterns with objects:
button, rock, button, rock, button, rock, __?__, __?__

Patterns with shapes:

Patterns with sounds:
snap, clap, clap, snap, clap, clap, __?__, __?__, __?__

Patterns with motions:
bend left and up, bend left and up, stretch up,
bend left and up, bend left and up, stretch up,
__?__, __?__, __?__

You can do several repetitions of each pattern.

Thank you for helping your child discover the patterns in our world!

Sincerely,
Your child's teacher

Find and Make New Patterns **99**

Estimada familia:

Su niño está empezando a ver y explorar patrones que se encuentran en el mundo que los rodea. Los patrones son objetos, figuras, símbolos, sonidos o movimientos del cuerpo que se repiten y que aparecen una y otra vez en el mismo orden.

Su niño está aprendiendo patrones sencillos. Éstos irán evolucionando y haciéndose más complejos a lo largo del año. Los niños observan o crean un patrón cuando leen o dicen el patrón, de izquierda a derecha.

Usted puede ayudar a su niño a entender este concepto creando patrones en casa. Por ejemplo:

Patrones con objetos:
botón, piedra, botón, piedra, botón, piedra, _¿?_ , _¿?_

Patrones con figuras:

○ ○ ▭ ○ ○ ▭ ○ ○ ▭ , _¿?_ _¿?_

Patrones con sonidos:
chasquido, palmas, palmas, chasquido, palmas, palmas,
_¿?_ , _¿?_ , _¿?_

Patrones con movimientos:
inclínate hacia la izquierda y levántate, inclínate hacia la izquierda y levántate, estírate hacia arriba, inclínate hacia la izquierda, inclínate hacia la izquierda, estírate hacia arriba, _¿?_ , _¿?_ , _¿?_

¡Gracias por ayudar a su niño a descubrir los patrones de nuestro mundo!

Atentamente,
El maestro de su niño

Find and Make New Patterns

Write the number 10.

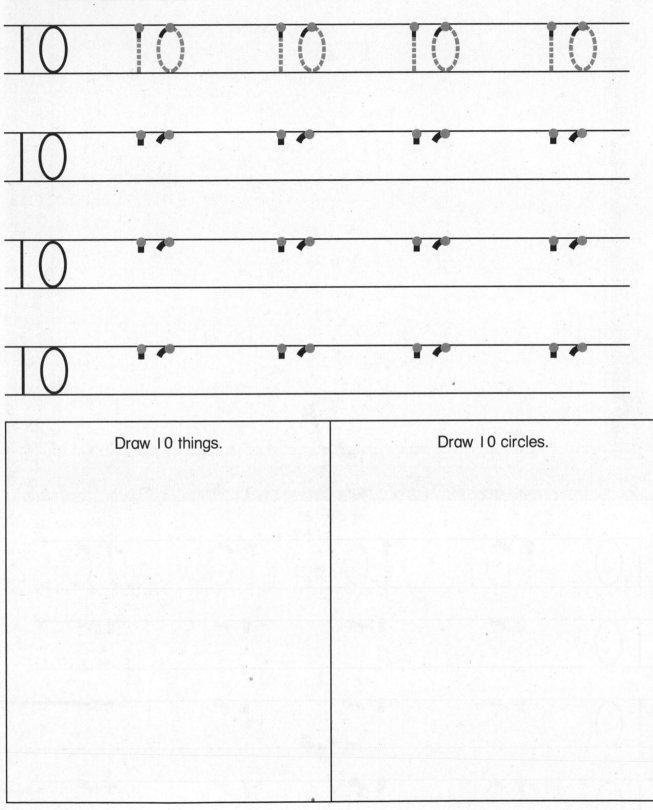

Draw 10 things.	Draw 10 circles.

On the Back Draw 10 fish in a pond. Then practice writing the number 10.

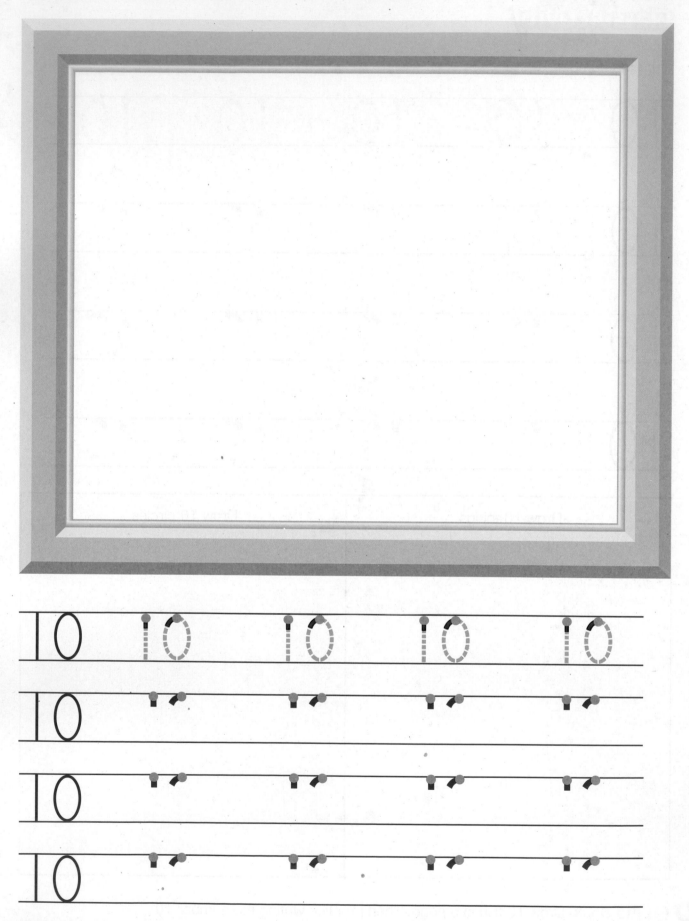

Addition and Subtraction Stories: Family Experience

Class Activity

Name _____

Use a pencil or marker and trace each number 2 times. Use the color red to trace the 8s and the color blue to trace the 9s.

| 8 | ● ● ● ● ●
 ● ● ● |
| 9 | ● ● ● ● ●
 ● ● ● ● ● |

8
9
8
8
9
8
9
9
9
8
9
8
8
8
9
8
9
8
8
9
8
9
8
9
8
8
9
9
9
8
8
9
8
9
8
9
8

Write the numbers 1–10.

➡ **On the Back** Write the numbers 1–10 in different sizes.

Number Writing Practice

Going Further

Name _____

Connect the dots in order.

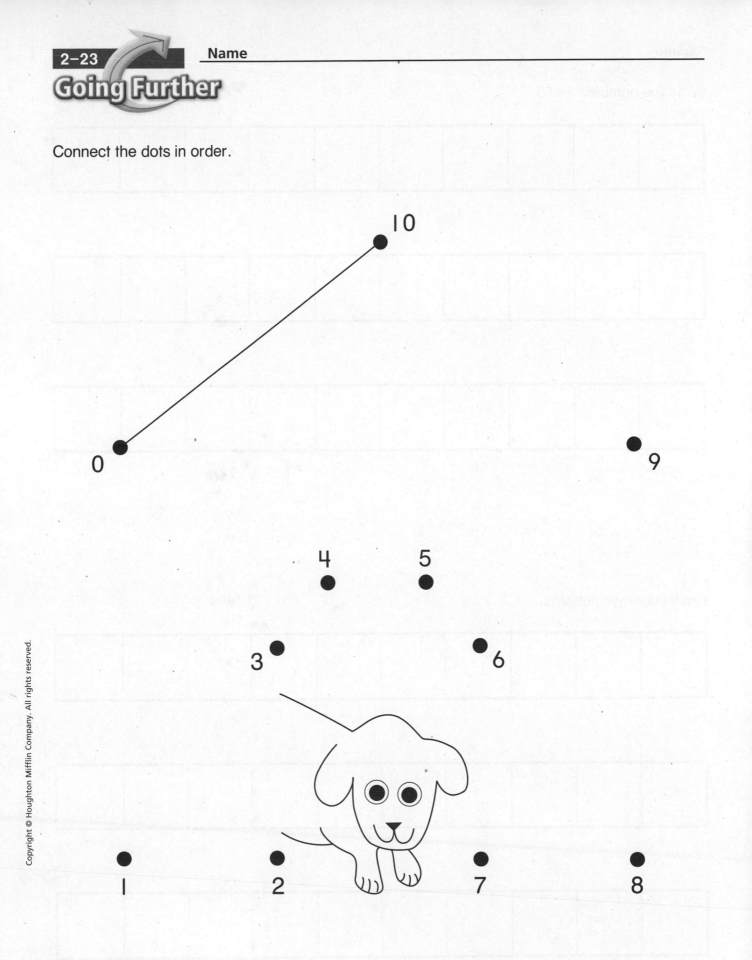

On the Back Write the numbers 1 through 10, and draw patterns.

More Numbers 1 Through 10: the −1 Pattern **105**

Write the numbers 1–10.

Draw your own patterns.

More Numbers 1 Through 10: the −1 Pattern

Name _____

Color each different kind of shape a different color.

Count the number of each shape in the picture.

Write the number.

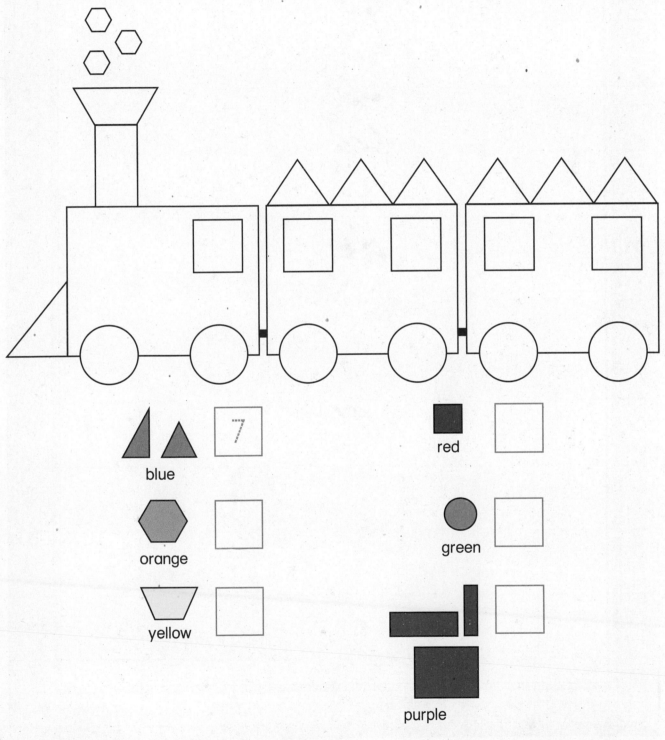

blue

orange

yellow

red

green

purple

➡ **On the Back** Draw your own scene with shapes.

Shapes in a Train Scene

Going Further

Name _____

Continue each **pattern**.

→ **On the Back** Draw your own patterns.

Shapes in a Train Scene **109**

Write the numbers 1–10.

Draw your own patterns.

Shapes in a Train Scene

Unit Test 2

Name _____

Exercises 1–2. Ring groups of the number. X out groups that are not the number.

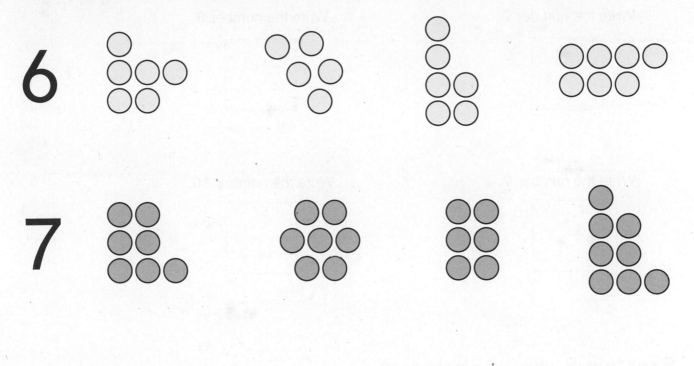

Exercises 3–4. Connect the dots in order. Use straight lines.

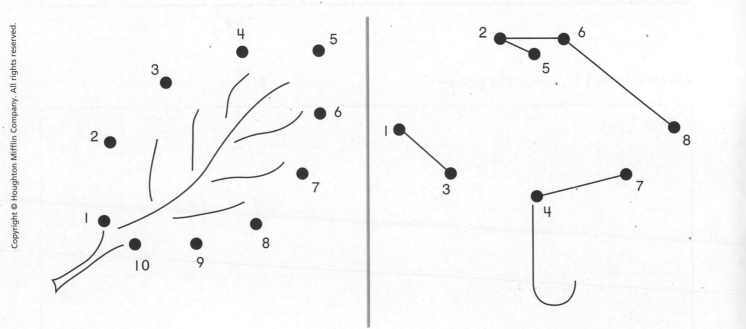

2 Unit Test

Name _____

Exercises 5–8. Write the numbers.

Write the number 7.

Write the number 8.

Write the number 9.

Write the number 10.

Exercise 9. Write the numbers 1–10.

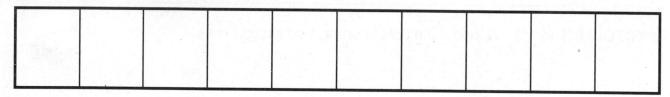

Exercise 10. Draw the picture.

Draw 7 fish.

Exercise 11. Draw the picture.

Draw 9 balloons.

Exercises 12–15. Continue the pattern.

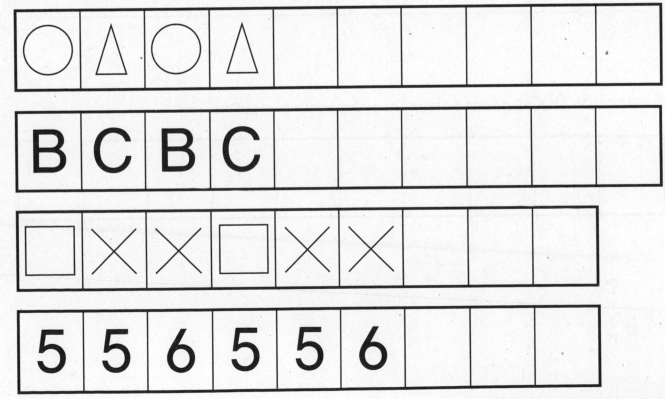

Exercises 16–19. Draw the shapes.

Draw 1 triangle.	Draw 2 squares.
Draw 3 circles.	Draw 4 rectangles.

Exercise 20. **Extended Response** Draw your own pattern.

Color each group of 1 through 10 a different color.

On the Back Draw 3 ducks on a pond and 2 ducks on the grass.

Numbers 1–10 and Math Stories: Park Scene

Dear Family:

Your child is starting a new unit on grouping concepts. These concepts provide a foundation for understanding basic math equations. In class, children will learn to find the ten in teen numbers (17 = 10 + 7), break apart numbers to find "partners" (6 = 4 + 2), recognize when numbers are equal or unequal, apply the concepts of *more* and *fewer*, and observe different attributes of shapes.

Being able to group numbers and shapes makes them easier to understand. You can help your child by practicing grouping concepts at home. Here is an example of an activity you can do with your child:

When cleaning up from play, have your child sort the objects before putting them away. Talk about the differences in size, shape, and color, and help your child place the items in groups based on these attributes. For example, the blocks below are sorted by size. They could also be sorted by color.

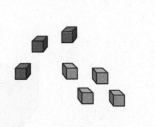 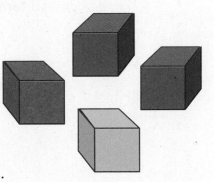

In Unit 2 your child did patterns of the forms ABAB, ABBABB, and AABAAB. In this unit they will also begin doing patterns of the form ABCABC. Work with your child to make patterns with objects and sounds and body motions.

Thank you for your continued support.

Sincerely,
Your child's teacher

Estimada familia:

Su niño está empezando una nueva unidad sobre los conceptos de agrupar. Estos conceptos son la base para comprender las ecuaciones matemáticas básicas. Los niños aprenderán a hallar la decena en los números del 11 al 19 ($17 = 10 + 7$), a separar números para hallar "partes" ($6 = 4 + 2$), a reconocer si los números son iguales o no, a aplicar los conceptos de *más* y *menos* y a fijarse en las características de las figuras.

Agrupar números y figuras los hace más fáciles de entender. Usted puede ayudar a su niño practicando en casa los conceptos de agrupar. Aquí tiene un ejemplo de una actividad que puede hacer con su niño:

Cuando estén guardando las cosas después de jugar, pídale a su niño que ponga los objetos en categorías antes de guardarlos. Háblele de las diferencias de tamaño, forma y color, y ayúdelo a colocar los objetos en grupos según estas diferencias. Por ejemplo, los bloques que aparecen a continuación están agrupados según su tamaño. También se pueden agrupar según su color.

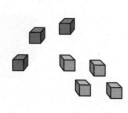 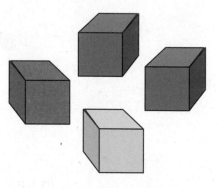

En la Unidad 2, su niño hizo patrones de las formas ABAB, ABBABB y AABAAB. En esta unidad también harán patrones de la forma ABCABC. Haga con su niño patrones con objetos, sonidos y movimientos.

Gracias por su apoyo.

Atentamente,
El maestro de su niño

Cut on dotted lines. **Fold** on solid lines and tape at top and bottom.

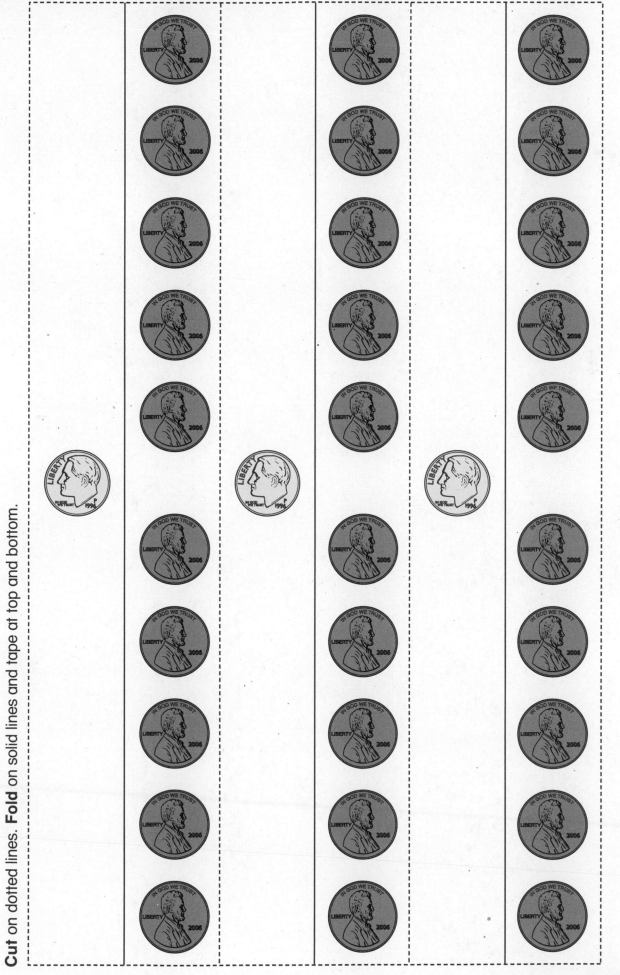

Dime Strips

Name

Connect the dots from 1 through 20 and color the Ten Bug.

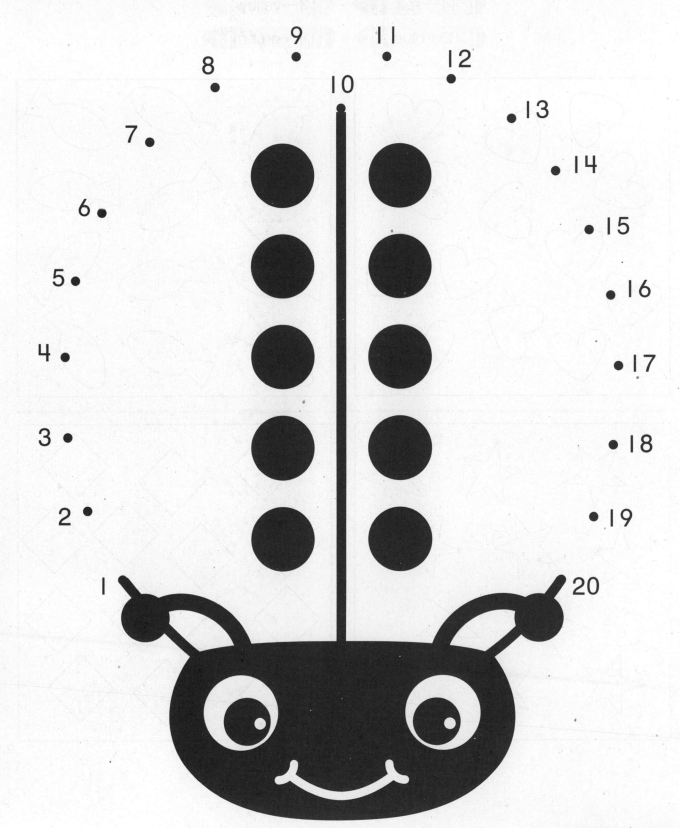

Name _____

Extra Practice

Ring a group of 10 in each box. Count and color the items. Use the colors shown.

11—red   13—yellow

12—blue   14—green

Groups of 10

Dear Family:

Your child is learning about partners of numbers. We call the number pairs that make up a number "partners" because they go together to make that number. For example,

6 has partners: 1 and 5   2 and 4   3 and 3

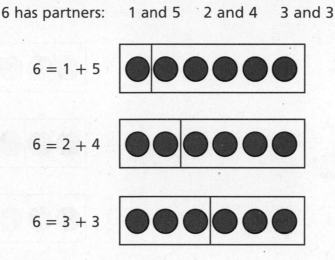

$6 = 1 + 5$

$6 = 2 + 4$

$6 = 3 + 3$

The partner idea is very important for understanding numbers. It will help your child understand addition and subtraction. You can help your child see partners in everyday life. When you have a small number of objects, for example, 5 crackers, you can ask your child to make the partners of 5. Your child can show 1 and 4 crackers and can also show 2 and 3 crackers. Doing this often with different objects will help your child understand numbers.

Thank you!

Sincerely,
Your child's teacher

Explore Partners Through 6 **123**

Estimada familia:

Su niño está aprendiendo sobre las partes de los números. Llamamos "partes" a la pareja de números que componen un número porque se unen para formar ese número. Por ejemplo,

6 tiene las partes: 1 y 5   2 y 4   3 y 3

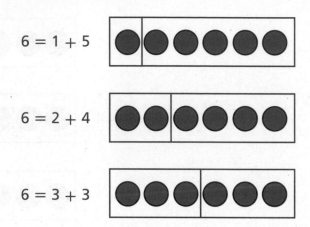

6 = 1 + 5

6 = 2 + 4

6 = 3 + 3

La idea de las partes es muy importante para entender los números. Eso ayudará a su niño a entender la suma y la resta. Ud. puede ayudar a su niño a ver las partes en la vida diaria. Cuando tiene un pequeño número de objetos, por ejemplo 5 galletas, puede pedirle a su niño que muestre las partes de 5. Su niño puede mostrar 1 galleta y 4 galletas y también 2 galletas y 3 galletas. Hacer esto a menudo con distintos objetos puede ayudar a su niño a entender los números.

¡Gracias!

Atentamente,
El maestro de su niño

Class Activity

Name _____

Write the number.

1.

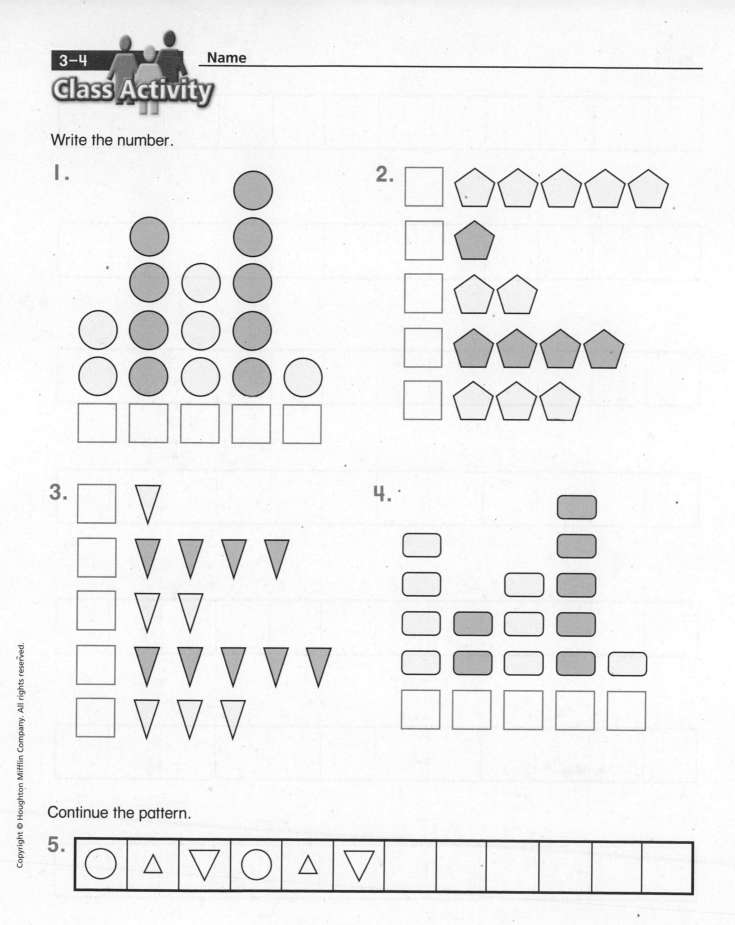

2.

3.

4.

Continue the pattern.

5.

➡ **On the Back** Draw your own patterns.

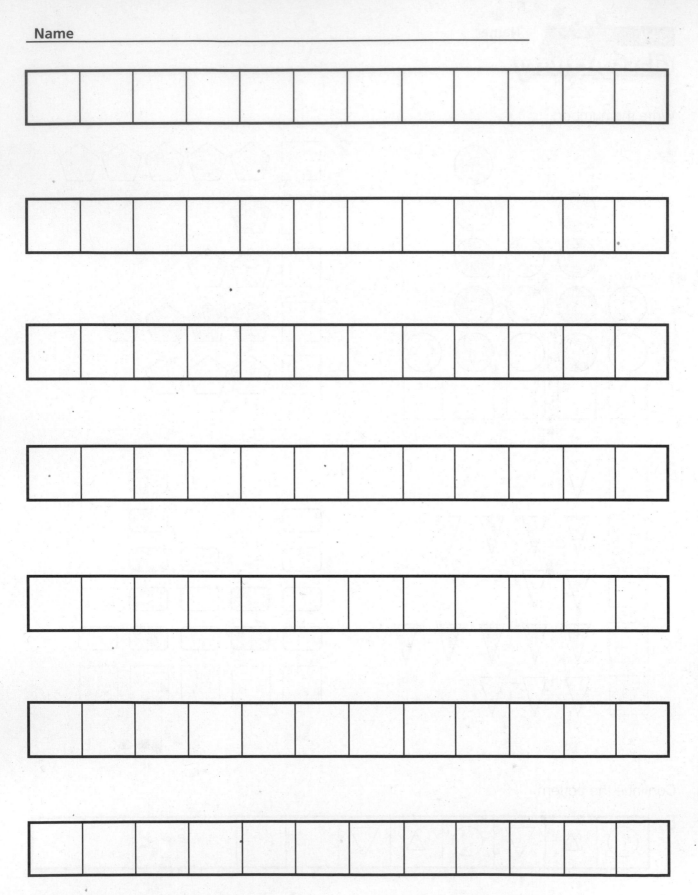

Addition and Subtraction Stories: Park Scene

1. Draw the circles on the Number Parade. Use a 5-group.

6	7	8	9	10

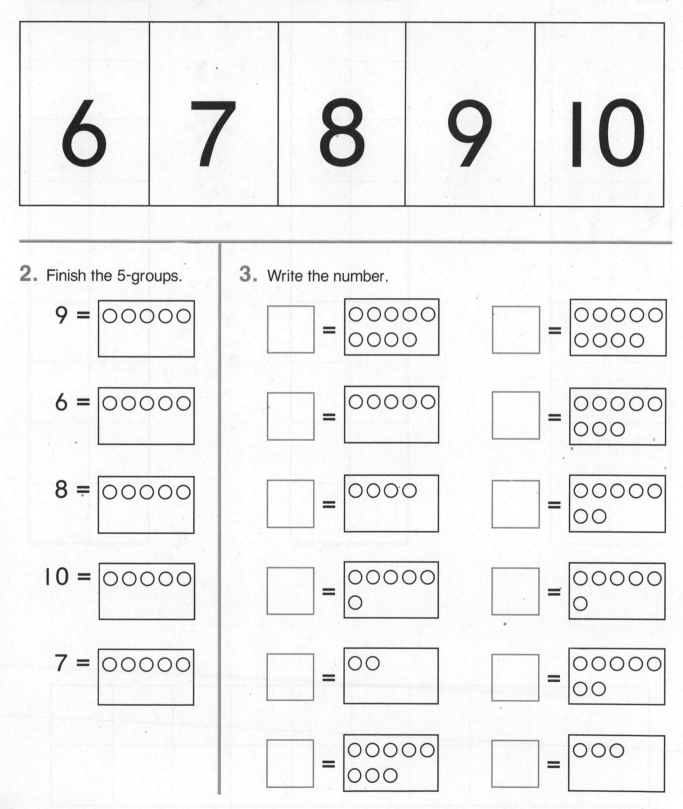

2. Finish the 5-groups.

9 = ⬚ OOOOO

6 = ⬚ OOOOO

8 = ⬚ OOOOO

10 = ⬚ OOOOO

7 = ⬚ OOOOO

3. Write the number.

☐ = OOOOO OOOO

☐ = OOOOO

☐ = OOOO

☐ = OOOOO O

☐ = OO

☐ = OOOOO OOO

☐ = OOOOO OOOO

☐ = OOOOO OOO

☐ = OOOOO OO

☐ = OOOOO O

☐ = OOOOO OO

☐ = OOO

➡ **On the Back** Write the numbers 1–20.

1	11
2	12
3	13
4	14
5	15
6	16
7	17
8	18
9	19
10	20

1	11
10	20

More Groups of 10

Dear Family:

When children first start counting, they count objects one at a time. Helping children see 5-groups and 10-groups enables them to understand larger (greater) numbers. We are learning that if we can see groups of objects as 5-groups and 10-groups, then we can understand greater numbers. Children learn to make these groups with objects. Later they will see them as organized groups in their minds.

Your child is learning that the teen numbers 11, 12, 13, 14, 15, 16, 17, 18, 19, and 20 each have one 10 inside: $11 = 10 + 1$, $12 = 10 + 2$, and so on through $19 = 10 + 9$, $20 = 10 + 10$.

Have your child practice counting groups of objects. Your child can find and separate the 10-group from the total quantity to see the 10 hiding inside the teen number.

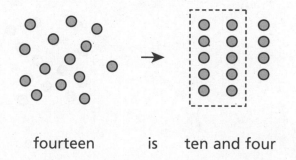

fourteen   is   ten and four

Your child can then show this number by using the number cards on the next page.

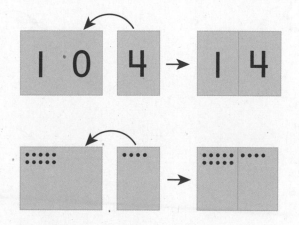

Thank you for your cooperation!

Sincerely,
Your child's teacher

Estimada familia:

Cuando los niños empiezan a contar, suelen contar los objetos uno por uno. Ayudarlos a ver los objetos en grupos de 5 y grupos de 10, les facilita el aprendizaje de números más grandes (mayores). Estamos aprendiendo que si podemos ver grupos de objetos como grupos de 5 y grupos de 10, entonces podemos entender números más grandes. Los niños aprenden a formar estos grupos con objetos. Más adelante los verán mentalmente como grupos organizados.

Su niño está aprendiendo que los números 11, 12, 13, 14, 15, 16, 17, 18, 19 y 20 tienen un 10: 11 = 10 + 1, 12 = 10 + 2, y así sucesivamente, hasta 19 = 10 + 9, 20 = 10 + 10.

Pida a su niño que practique contando grupos de objetos. Su niño puede separar el grupo de 10 de la cantidad total, para ver el 10 escondido en los números del 11 al 20.

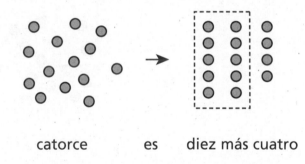

catorce   es   diez más cuatro

Después, su niño puede mostrar este número usando las tarjetas de números de la página siguiente.

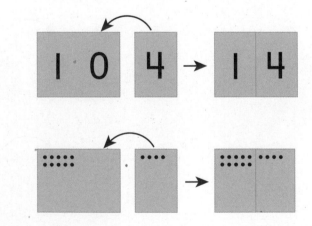

¡Gracias por su colaboración!

Atentamente,
El maestro de su niño

Tarjetas de números para practicar en casa

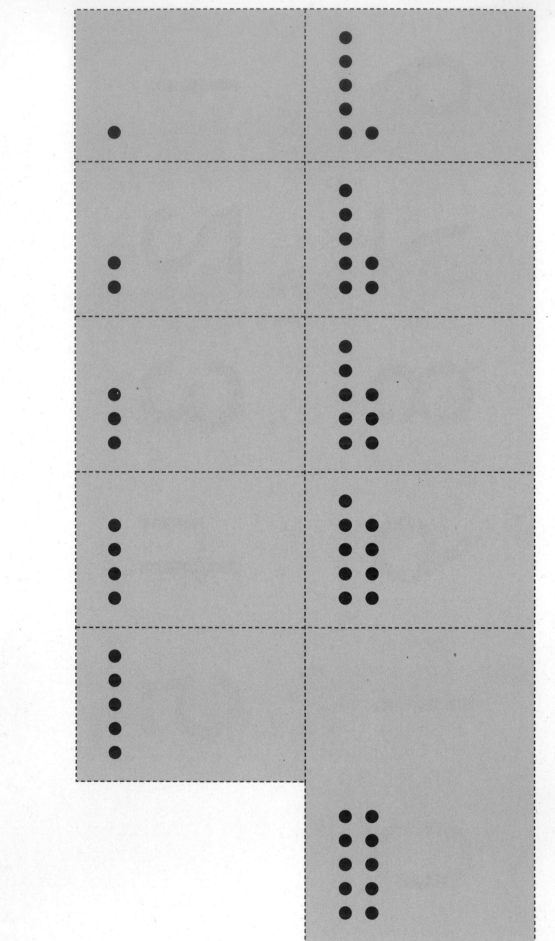

More Groups of 10

Class Activity

Write the number **pattern** in each row.

1.

★★★	★★★★	★★★★★	★★★	★★★★	★★★★★	★★★	★★★★	★★★★★
3	4	5	3	4	5	3	4	5

Write the number.

2.

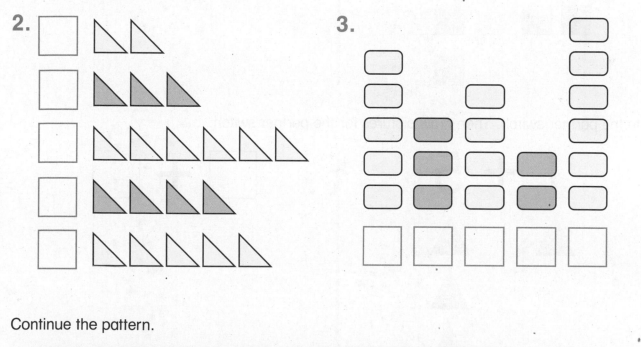

3.

Continue the pattern.

4.

Going Further

Vocabulary
switch the partners

Name

Draw pictures for **switching the partners**.

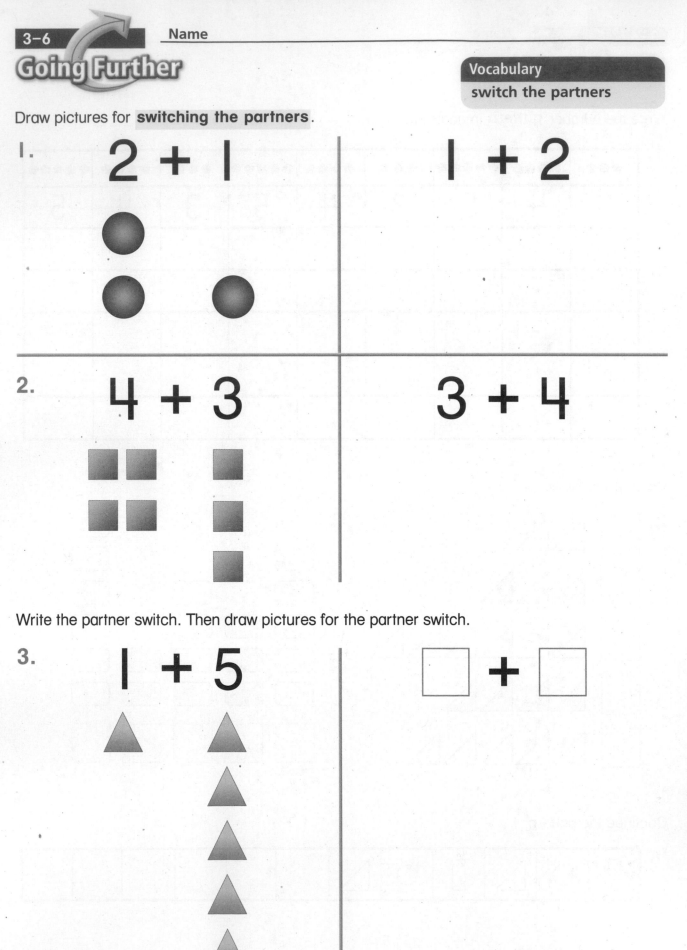

1. 2 + 1   1 + 2

2. 4 + 3   3 + 4

Write the partner switch. Then draw pictures for the partner switch.

3. 1 + 5   ☐ + ☐

Explore Partners Through 6 with Pennies

Dear Family:

Some Unit 3 homework pages will ask children to extend a number pattern. The numbers on the top row follow a repeating pattern. Children are to "read" (say) and copy the pattern from left to right.

••	•••	••••	•••••	••	•••	••••	•••••
2	3	4	5	2	3	4	5
2	3	4	5	2	3	4	5
2	3	4	5	2	3	4	5

Children in many other countries learn to write small numbers. It is easier for most children to write smaller. Learning to write neatly is important.

Please help your child learn to write numbers. This will take time and practice. Be supportive and encourage your child.

Thank you!

Sincerely,
Your child's teacher

Estimada familia:

En algunas de las hojas de tarea de la Unidad 3, se pedirá a los niños que aumenten un patrón numérico. Los números de la primera fila siguen un patrón que se repite. Los niños deben "leer" (decir) y copiar el patrón de izquierda a derecha.

••	•••	••••	•••••	••	•••	••••	•••••
2	3	4	5	2	3	4	5
2	3	4	5	2	3	4	5
2	3	4	5	2	3	4	5

Los niños de muchos otros países aprenden a escribir números pequeños. Para la mayoría de los niños es más fácil escribir con letra pequeña. Es importante aprender a escribir bien.

Por favor ayude a su niño a escribir los números. Esto requiere tiempo y práctica. Anímelo y dele su apoyo.

¡Gracias!

Atentamente,
El maestro de su niño

Explore Partners Through 6 with Pennies

Class Activity

Name _____

Vocabulary
5-group

1. Draw the circles on the Number Parade. Use a **5-group**.

6	7	8	9	10

2. Finish the 5-groups.

6 = ⭘⭘⭘⭘⭘

7 = ⭘⭘⭘⭘

8 = ⭘⭘⭘⭘⭘

9 = ⭘⭘⭘⭘⭘

10 = ⭘⭘⭘⭘⭘

3. Write the number.

☐ = ⭘⭘⭘

☐ = ⭘⭘⭘⭘⭘⭘

☐ = ⭘⭘

☐ = ⭘⭘⭘⭘⭘⭘⭘⭘

☐ = ⭘⭘⭘⭘⭘⭘

☐ = ⭘⭘⭘⭘⭘⭘⭘⭘

☐ = ⭘⭘⭘⭘⭘⭘⭘

☐ = ⭘⭘⭘⭘⭘

☐ = ⭘⭘⭘⭘⭘⭘

☐ = ⭘⭘⭘⭘⭘⭘⭘⭘⭘

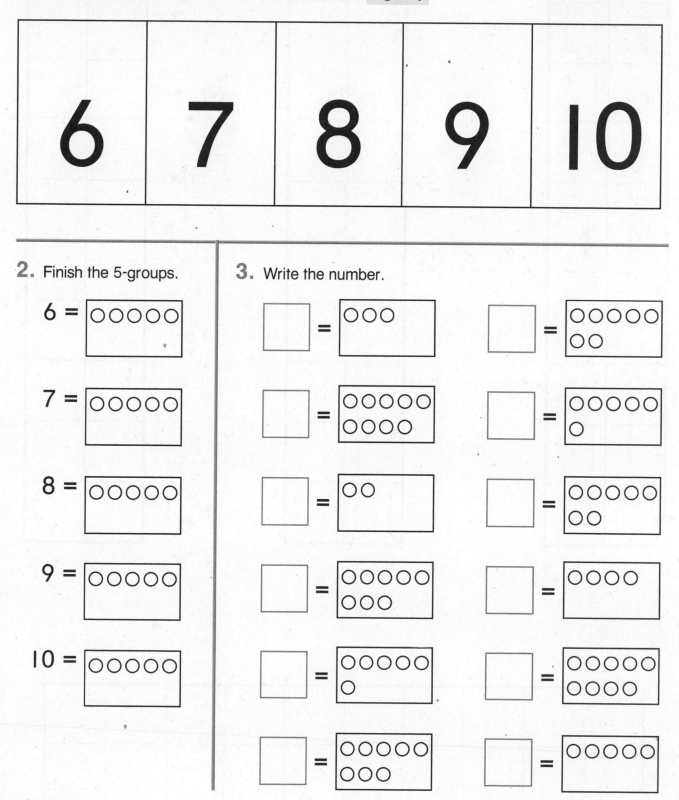

➡ **On the Back** Write the numbers 1–20.

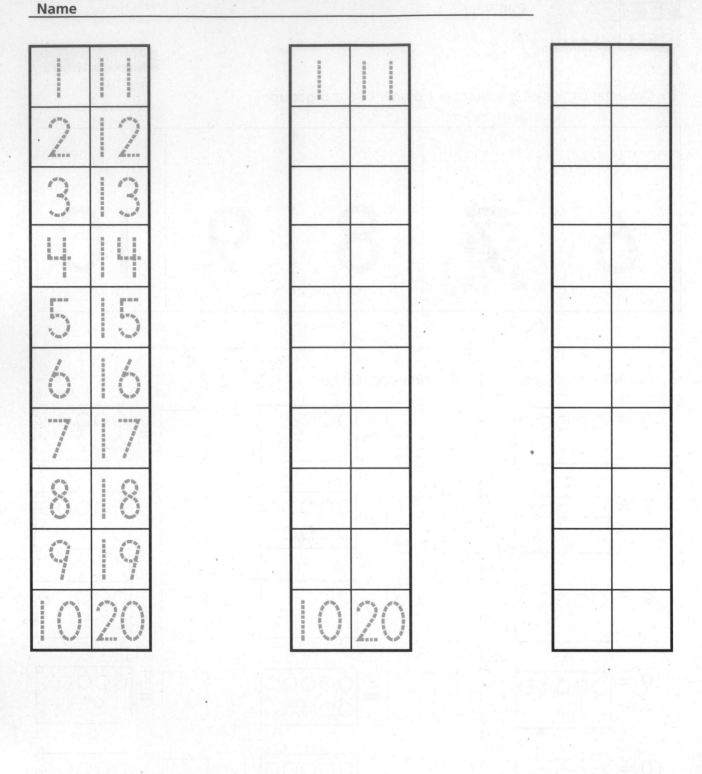

More Addition and Subtraction Stories: Park Scene

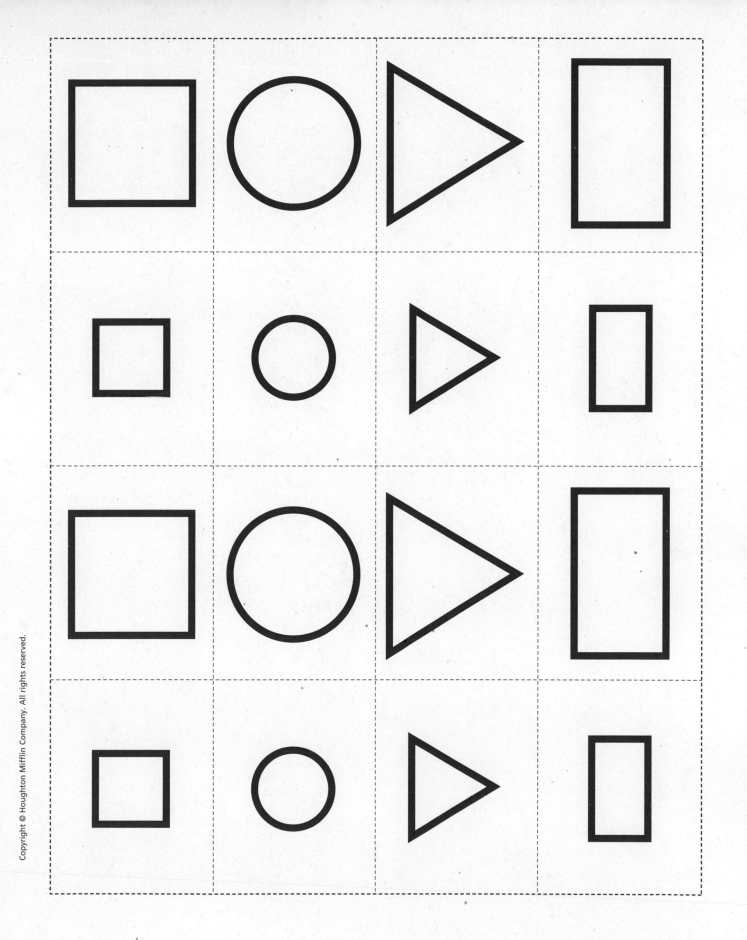

UNIT 3 LESSON 10

Attribute Cards **139**

Attribute Cards

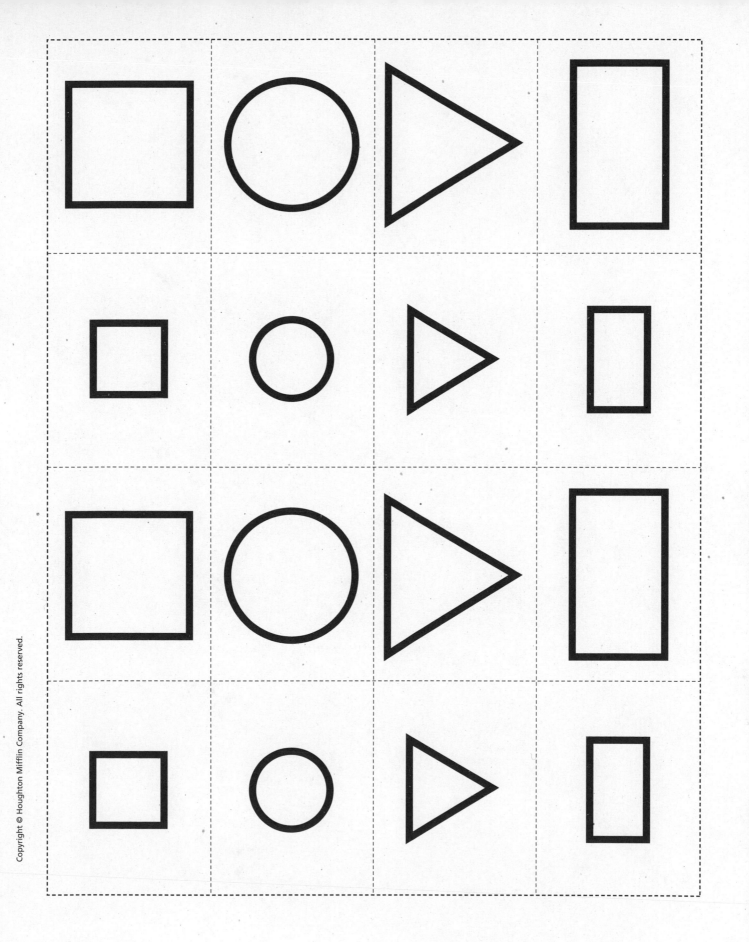

Attribute Cards **141**

Attribute Cards

Class Activity

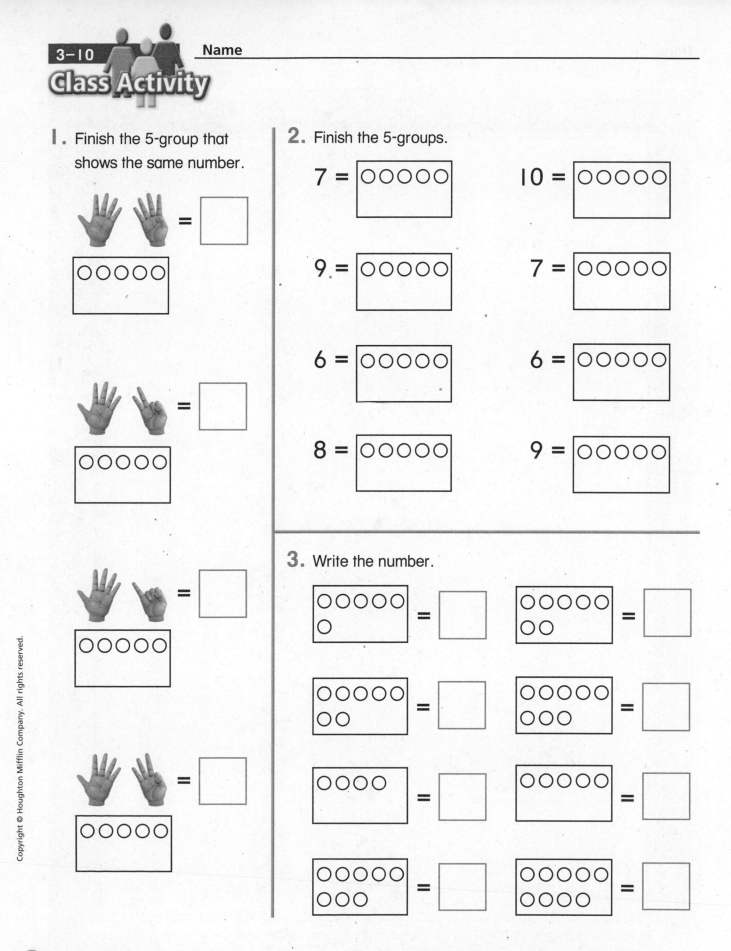

1. Finish the 5-group that shows the same number.

2. Finish the 5-groups.

7 = ◯◯◯◯◯

10 = ◯◯◯◯◯

9 = ◯◯◯◯◯

7 = ◯◯◯◯◯

6 = ◯◯◯◯◯

6 = ◯◯◯◯◯

8 = ◯◯◯◯◯

9 = ◯◯◯◯◯

3. Write the number.

On the Back Show a 5-group by drawing a hand with 5 fingers.

Explore Attributes: Shape, Size, and Color

Dear Family:

We want children to see numbers 6, 7, 8, 9, and 10 as having a 5 and some more. We call this using a 5-group. *This visual pattern will help children add and subtract and understand numbers.* It will also help later in calculations with larger (greater) numbers.

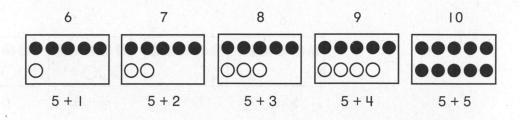

The 5-groups can be shown all across or up and down.

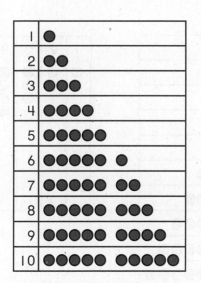

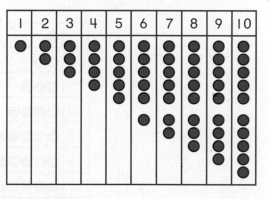

Help your child see 5-groups in numbers. Use pennies and arrange numbers in 5-groups.

Thank you!

Sincerely,
Your child's teacher

Estimada familia:

Queremos que los niños vean el 6, el 7, el 8, el 9 y el 10 como números que tienen un 5 y algo más. A esto lo llamamos usar un grupo de 5. *Este patrón visual ayudará a los niños a sumar y restar y a entender los números.* También será una ayuda más adelante para hacer cálculos con números más grandes (mayores).

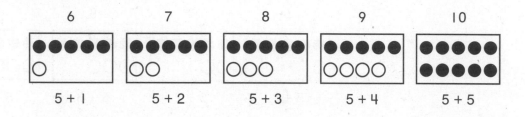

Los grupos de 5 se pueden presentar de manera horizontal o de manera vertical.

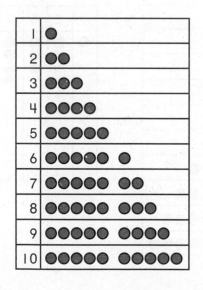

Ayude a su niño a ver grupos de 5 en los números. Use monedas de un centavo y organice los números en grupos de 5.

¡Gracias!

Atentamente,
El maestro de su niño

Explore Attributes: Shape, Size, and Color

Class Activity

Name _____

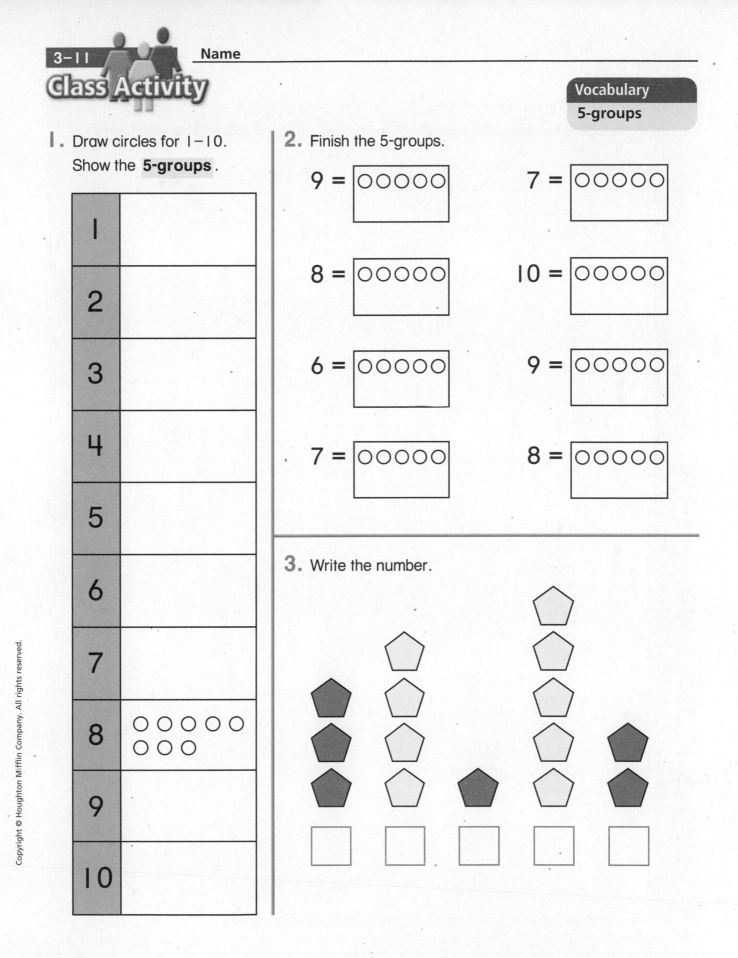

Vocabulary

5-groups

1. Draw circles for 1–10.
Show the **5-groups**.

1	
2	
3	
4	
5	
6	
7	
8	○ ○ ○ ○ ○ ○ ○ ○
9	
10	

2. Finish the 5-groups.

9 = ○○○○○

7 = ○○○○○

8 = ○○○○○

10 = ○○○○○

6 = ○○○○○

9 = ○○○○○

7 = ○○○○○

8 = ○○○○○

3. Write the number.

On the Back Write the numbers 1–10 in all different sizes.

Practice Addition and Subtraction Stories: Park Scene

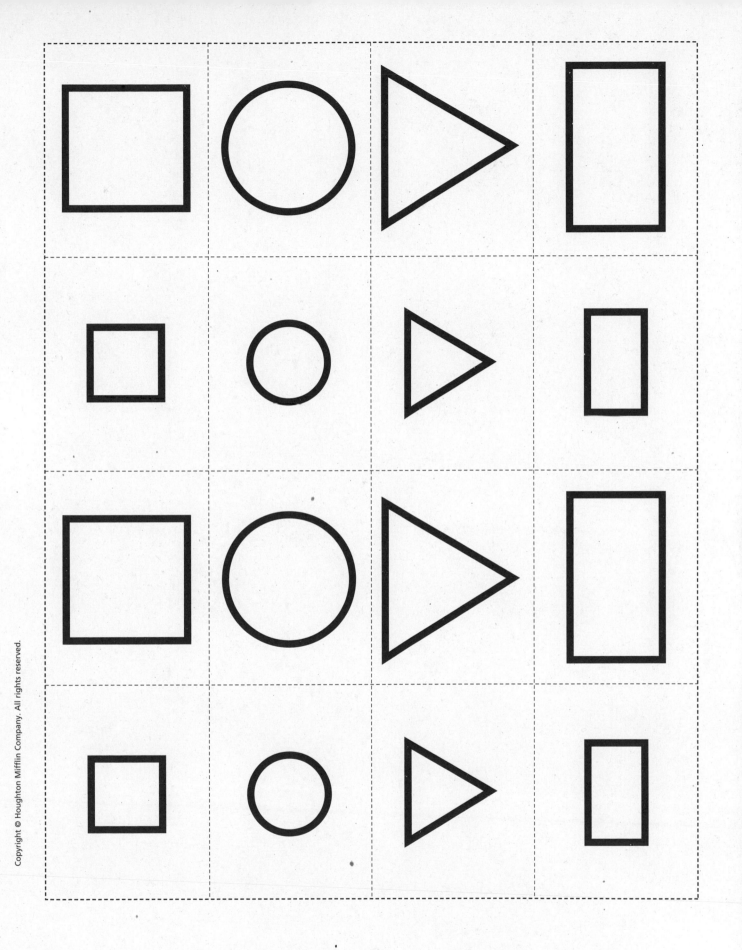

Attribute Cards

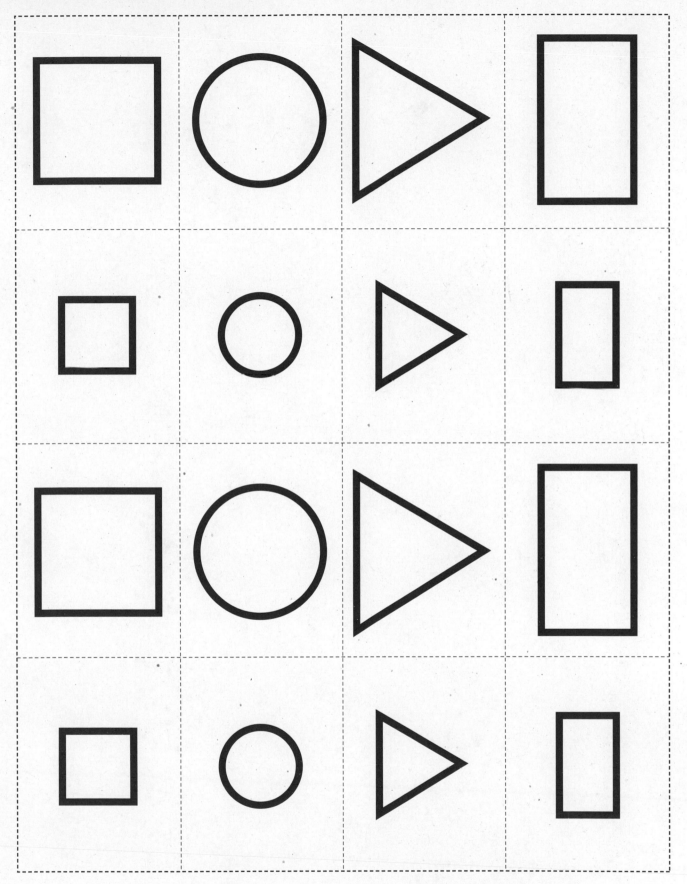

Attribute Cards **151**

Attribute Cards

Name _____

Class Activity

Vocabulary

equals sign (=)
is not equal to sign (≠)

1. Draw circles for 1–10. Show the 5-group.

1	2	3	4	5	6	7	8	9	10
								○○○○○ ○○○○	

2. Write each number and an **equals sign (=)** or an **is not equal to sign (≠)**.

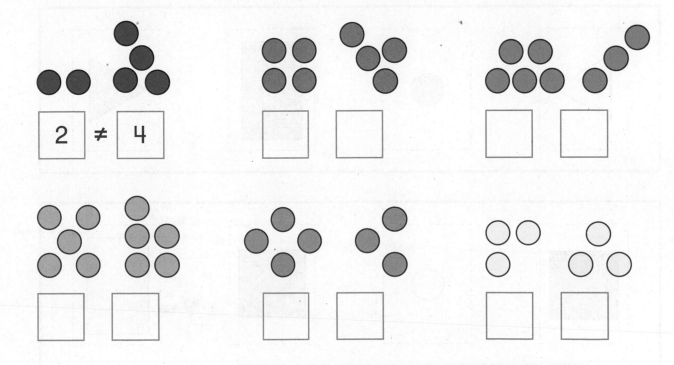

$2 \ne 4$

More Attributes: Shape, Size, and Color **153**

Going Further

Name _____

Draw an X through the shape that does not belong.

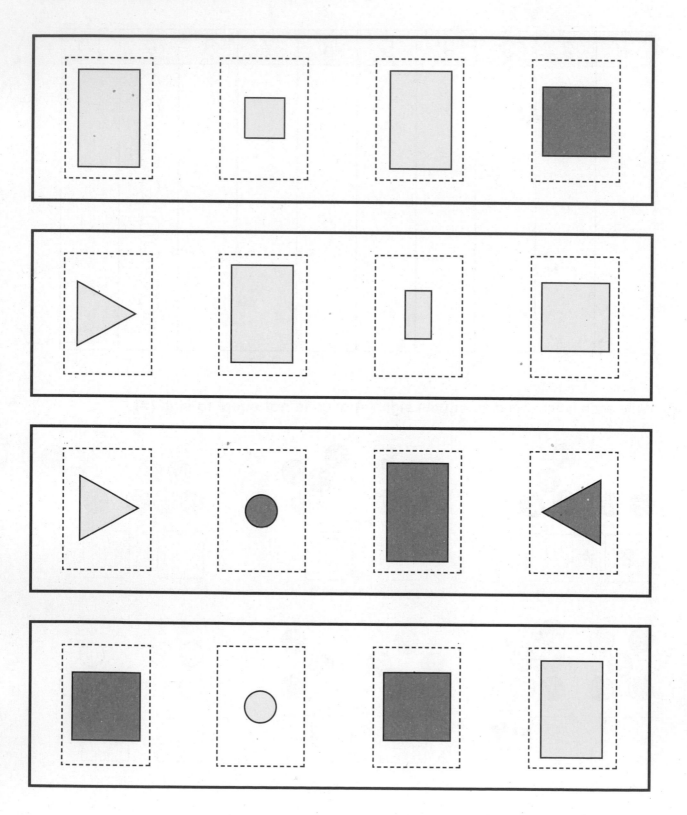

More Attributes: Shape, Size, and Color

Name _____

Vocabulary

equals sign (=)
is not equal to sign (≠)

1. Draw circles for 1–10. Show the 5-group.

1	2	3	4	5	6	7	8	9	10
							○○○○○ ○○○		

2. Write each number and an **equals sign (=)** or an **is not equal to sign (≠)**.

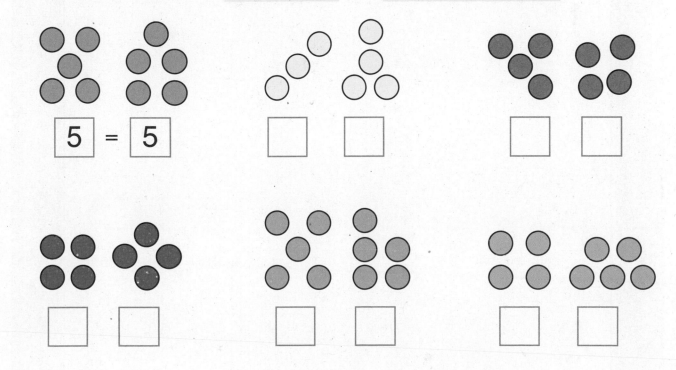

| 5 | = | 5 |

On the Back Draw 2 groups of circles. Write each number and = or ≠.

Attribute Card Activities

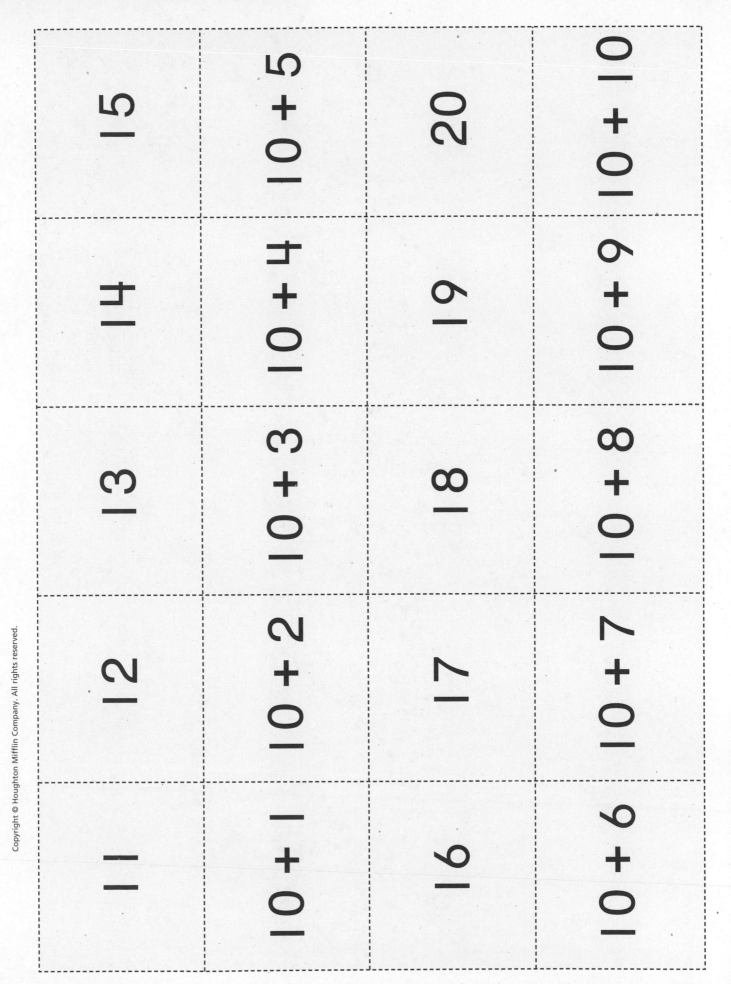

15	14	13	12	11
10 + 5	10 + 4	10 + 3	10 + 2	10 + 1
20	19	18	17	16
10 + 10	10 + 9	10 + 8	10 + 7	10 + 6

Teen Total Cards **157**

Class Activity

Name _____

Vocabulary
more
fewer

Draw some suns.

Draw some clouds.

Tell which has **more** and which has **fewer**.

Draw some square crackers.

Draw some round crackers.

Tell which has more and which has fewer.

Graph Drawings: Match and Compare **159**

Extra Practice

Name _____

1. Color the group with **more** pails blue.

   Color the group with **fewer** pails yellow.

   ◀| blue |▶

   ◀| yellow |▶

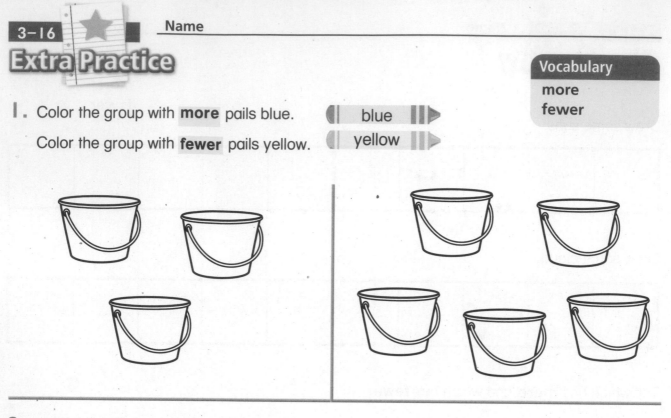

2. Color the group with more shovels blue.

   Color the group with fewer shovels yellow.

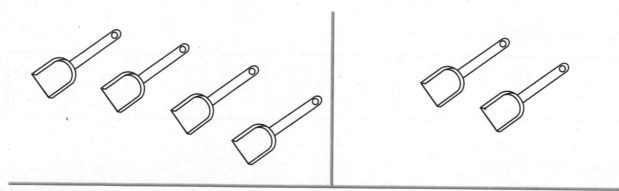

3. Color the group with more beach balls blue.

   Color the group with fewer beach balls yellow.

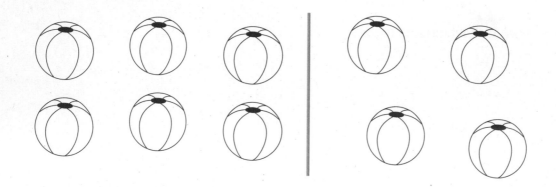

Graph Drawings: Match and Compare

Class Activity

Name _____

Vocabulary

partners

Write the **partners**.

5

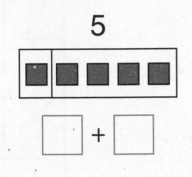

☐ + ☐

5

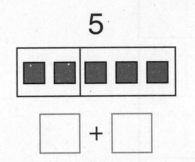

☐ + ☐

6

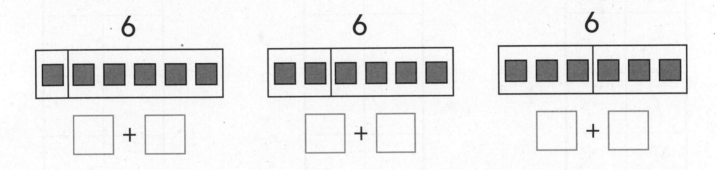

☐ + ☐   ☐ + ☐   ☐ + ☐

4

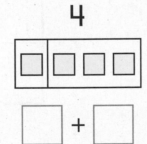

☐ + ☐

4

☐ + ☐

3

☐ + ☐

2

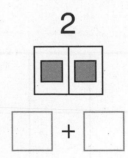

☐ + ☐

➡ On the Back Write the numbers 1–20.

1	11
2	12
3	13
4	14
5	15
6	16
7	17
8	18
9	19
10	20

1	11
10	20

2- and 3-Dimensional Shapes: Squares and Cubes

Class Activity

Write the **partners**.

6

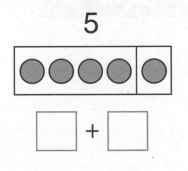

☐ + ☐

6

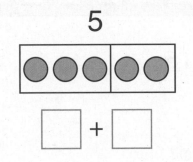

☐ + ☐

6

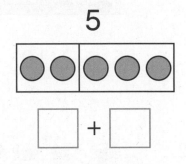

☐ + ☐

5

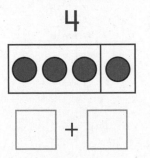

☐ + ☐

5

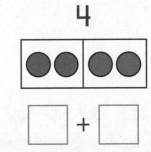

☐ + ☐

5

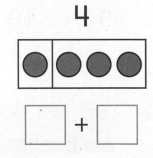

☐ + ☐

4

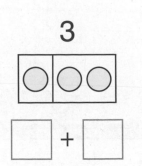

☐ + ☐

4

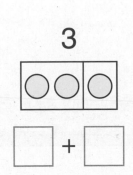

☐ + ☐

4

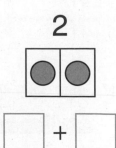

☐ + ☐

3

☐ + ☐

3

☐ + ☐

2

☐ + ☐

Going Further

Name _____

Vocabulary

estimate

Look at the teddy bears on the shelf. There are 10 teddy bears.
Then use what you see to **estimate**.

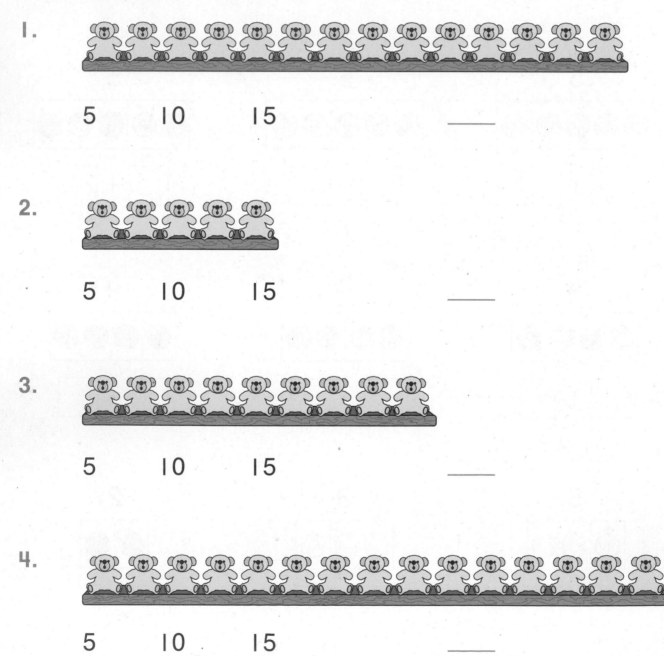

10

Estimate how many teddy bears. Ring 5, 10, or 15. Then count and write the
number of teddy bears.

1.

    5   10   15   _____

2.

    5   10   15   _____

3.

    5   10   15   _____

4.

    5   10   15   _____

Build Teen Numbers with Classroom Objects

Dear Family:

In the next 4 days, please find 20 of the same kind of small object that your child can take to school and paste onto a sheet of paper. For example, your child can use buttons or stickers, or you can cut out 20 small pieces of paper or fabric.

The objects will be used for an activity to help your child learn to see the 10 inside teen numbers: 11, 12, 13, 14, 15, 16, 17, 18, and 19.

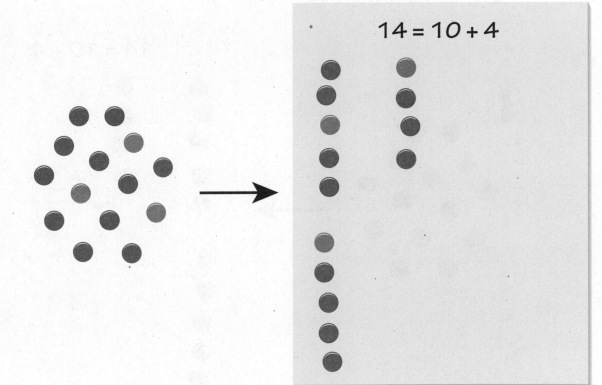

Thank you for your cooperation!

Sincerely,
Your child's teacher

Build Teen Numbers with Classroom Objects **165**

Estimada familia:

Durante los 4 días siguientes, por favor busque 20 objetos pequeños, del mismo tipo, que su niño pueda llevar a la escuela y pegar en una hoja de papel. Por ejemplo, su niño puede usar botones o figuras adhesivas, o usted puede cortar 20 pedacitos de papel o tela.

Los objetos se usarán en una actividad que ayudará a su niño a identificar el 10 en los números entre el 11 y el 19: 11, 12, 13, 14, 15, 16, 17, 18 y 19.

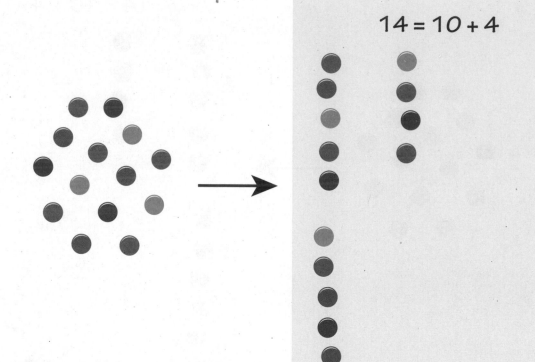

$$14 = 10 + 4$$

¡Gracias por su colaboración!

Atentamente,
El maestro de su niño

Build Teen Numbers with Classroom Objects

Name _____

Vocabulary

first	fourth
second	fifth
third	

Look at the children in line. See who is **first**, **second**, **third**, **fourth**, and **fifth**. Listen to the directions.

Color the rest of the page.

More Graph Drawings: Match and Compare **167**

Draw some triangles.

Draw some circles.

Tell which has **more** and which has **fewer** .

Draw some napkins.

Draw some bowls.

Tell which has more and which has fewer.

More Graph Drawings: Match and Compare

Extra Practice

Look at the children waiting in line. Talk about who is **first**, **second**, **third**, **fourth**, and **fifth**.

Vocabulary

first	fourth
second	fifth
third	

➡️ **On the Back** Draw a picture of three children in a line. Write 1, 2, and 3 to show who is first, second, and third.

More Graph Drawings: Match and Compare **169**

More Graph Drawings: Match and Compare

Name _____

Vocabulary
more
fewer

Draw some oranges.

Draw some pears.

Tell which has **more** and which has **fewer**.

Draw some bananas.

Draw some apples.

Tell which has more and which has fewer.

⮕ **On the Back** Write the numbers 1–20.

More Teen Numbers with Classroom Objects **171**

1	11
2	12
3	13
4	14
5	15
6	16
7	17
8	18
9	19
10	20

1	11
10	20

More Teen Numbers with Classroom Objects

Class Activity

Name _____

Draw circles for 1–10. Show the 5-group.

1	
2	
3	
4	
5	
6	
7	
8	○○○○○ ○○○
9	
10	

Write each number and = or ≠.

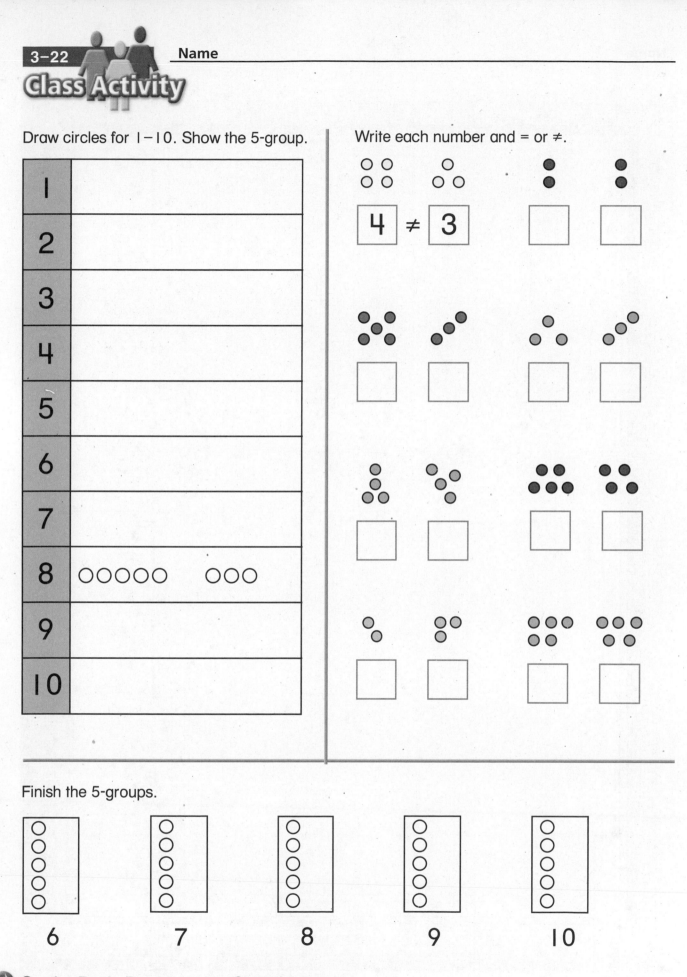

Finish the 5-groups.

6   7   8   9   10

On the Back Draw 8 circles. Show the 5-group.

More Attribute Card Activities

Draw the same picture in all 20 boxes.

Cut on dashed lines.

Object Collections: Teen Numbers **175**

Object Collections: Teen Numbers

Class Activity

Name _____

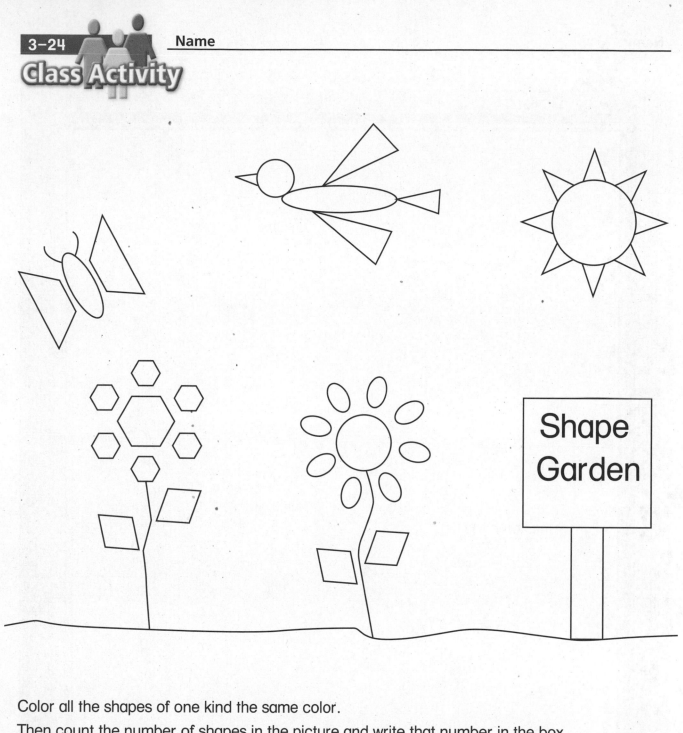

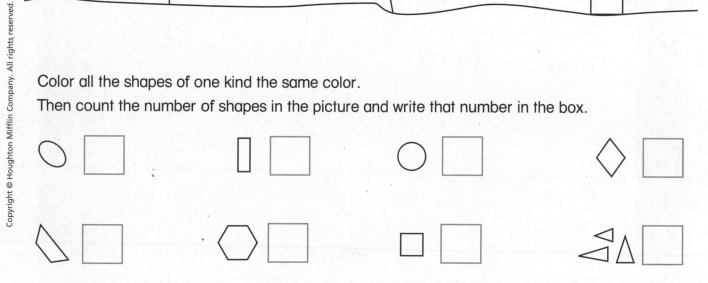

Color all the shapes of one kind the same color.

Then count the number of shapes in the picture and write that number in the box.

➡ **On the Back** Draw your own scene with shapes.

Shapes in a Garden Scene

Class Activity

1. Draw the legs on the other side of the praying mantis.
   Ring the addition for the number of legs on a praying mantis.

3 + 3   1 + 2   3 + 2

___

2. Draw the antennae on the other side of the ant.
   Ring the addition for the number of antennae an ant has.

1 + 2   2 + 2   1 + 1

___

3. Draw the wings on the other side of the dragonfly.
   Ring the addition for the number of wings a dragonfly has.

1 + 1   2 + 2   1 + 2

Name _____

1. Show how to share 12 crackers among 3 people.
Write how many crackers each person will get.

Each person will get _____ crackers.

2. Another person arrives. Now show how the
12 crackers can be shared among 4 people.
Write how many crackers each person will get.

Each person will get _____ crackers.

Use Mathematical Processes

3

Unit Test

Name _____

Exercises 1–3. Write the partners.

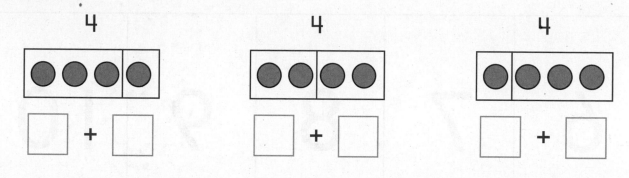

4   4   4

☐ + ☐   ☐ + ☐   ☐ + ☐

5   5   5

☐ + ☐   ☐ + ☐   ☐ + ☐

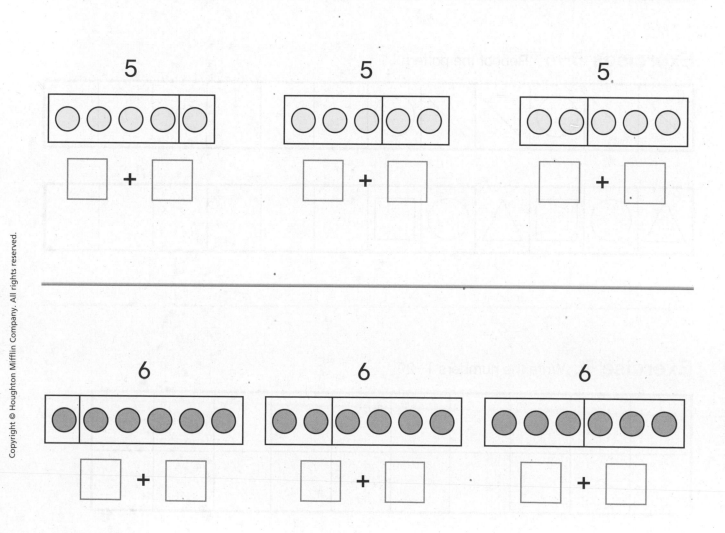

6   6   6

☐ + ☐   ☐ + ☐   ☐ + ☐

Name _____

Exercise 4. Draw the circles on the Number Parade. Use a 5-group.

6	7	8	9	10

Exercises 5–6. Repeat the pattern.

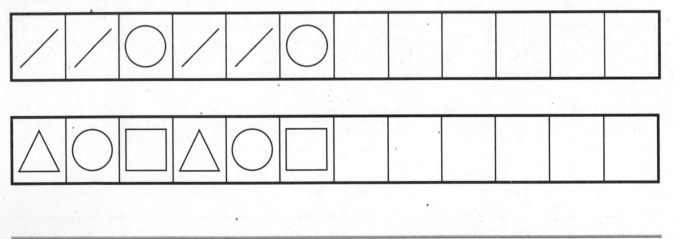

Exercise 7. Write the numbers 1–20.

Exercises 8–9. Write each number and = or ≠.

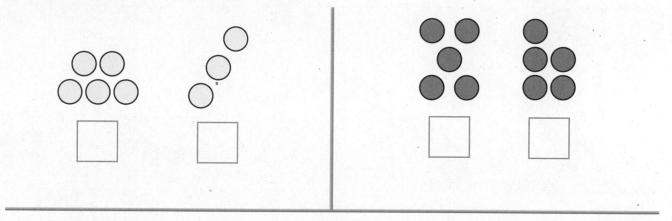

Exercise 10. Extended Response Draw 2 groups of triangles.

Write each number and = or ≠.